DARE TO STAND

Read and enjoy the book of Daniel

Dare to Stand Alone

Stuart Olyott

EVANGELICAL PRESS

EVANGELICAL PRESS
Faverdale North, Darlington, DL3 0PH, England

©Evangelical Press 1982

First published 1982
Second impression 1985
Third impression 1989
Fourth impression 1995
Fifth impression 2001

ISBN 0 85234 163 6

Printed in Great Britain by Creative Print & Design, Wales

DOLL

'Many women have done excellently,
but you surpass them all' (*Proverbs 31:29*).

CONTENTS

		Page
Introduction		9
1.	Setting the scene	11
2.	Off to Babylon!	16
3.	Nebuchadnezzar's dream	24
4.	The burning fiery furnace	37
5.	Nebuchadnezzar's turn	50
6.	How to be lost	63
7.	In the lions' den	74
8.	An intermission	86
9.	The vision of the four beasts	93
10.	The little horn	103
11.	A great prayer	115
12.	An old man sees a vision	129
13.	History is his story	140
14.	Antiochus Epiphanes!	150
15.	The end!	160
Thank you		171

Introduction

This book is for those who would like to read and enjoy the book of Daniel. If you want to read all the boring theories that scholars have dreamed up, you must look elsewhere. If you want convincing that Daniel was written in the sixth century B.C., and not in the second, as many writers now claim, your starting point should be E.J. Young's book mentioned on page 169. This book does not deal with such matters. Its aim is much more straightforward. It is to excite you to read Daniel for yourself, and to see what its message is for our times.

Daniel is basically a very easy book to understand. Its first six chapters are narrative. These are followed by six highly symbolic and apparently mysterious chapters, about which there has been considerable controversy. But they are not *that* difficult. The whole book is full of practical help — especially for believers who find themselves standing alone in the classroom or at work, or among their family and friends.

May the God of Daniel Himself draw near to us as we search His holy Word!

STUART OLYOTT,
Belvidere Road Church,
Liverpool.
1982.

1.
SETTING THE SCENE

The historical background

Long ago God chose one man — Abraham — and promised that through him and his seed all the families of the earth would be blessed.

The one man became a family, and the family became a nation. At last the nation went down to Egypt, where it remained for four hundred years.

Then it came out. You will have heard of the plagues, and the Passover, and the coming through the Red Sea. For forty years the nation, led by Moses, wandered in the wilderness, where it received God's law and instructions concerning the tabernacle, sacrifices and priesthood. When the wilderness wanderings were over, the nation came into the promised land, under the leadership of Joshua. Before he died the land had been largely conquered and divided among the twelve tribes.

This was followed by the period of the judges — men whom God raised up to deliver the nation from successive conquerors. Then came the period of the kings. The first king was Saul, who was followed in turn by David, Solomon and Rehoboam. All of these ruled over a united kingdom of twelve tribes.

Shortly after Rehoboam's reign began, the nation split into two. In the north was the kingdom of Israel (or Ephraim), and in the south the kingdom of Judah. The northern kingdom was composed of ten tribes and its capital was Samaria. The southern kingdom was composed of two tribes and its capital was Jerusalem. At first the two kingdoms were enemies. This was followed by a period of friendship, but eventually they were sworn enemies once more.

There were a number of different dynasties in the north, but no godly monarch ever sat on its throne. At last God moved to judge the nation, against whose apostasy He had often spoken by His prophets. The armies of mighty Assyria swept in from the north, and in 722 B.C. Samaria fell. The ten tribes of Israel were taken into captivity and disappeared from the face of the earth.

The southern kingdom continued for a further one hundred years. All its kings were of one dynasty and were descendants of David. The nation's life was one of increasing apostasy, and yet some of the kings were truly godly, and there were several periods of widespread spiritual awakening. In 609 B.C. Jehoiakim mounted the throne. His reign did nothing to arrest the prevailing idolatry and immorality, but rather increased it. The prophets warned that unless there was repentance there would be judgement, but their warnings went unheeded.

Over the horizon, in 605 B.C., came Nebuchadnezzar. Over the next twenty-three years, in four successive stages, he transported almost all the people of Judah to his native Babylon. By the rivers of Babylon they sat down and wept when they remembered Zion, and asked how they could sing the Lord's song in a strange land (Psalm 137:1,4).

The nation had turned a deaf ear to the warnings of God, and was now being left to the mercy of its enemies. However, within the apostate nation there remained a very small number of individuals who continued to be true to God, just as the prophets had predicted. This tiny remnant loved Him, and lived to please Him, even in distant Babylon. Such a remnant existed throughout the seventy years of exile. It is true that the nation as a whole wept idolatry out of its system. But loving allegiance to Jehovah was never the experience of more than a few. After the exile the remnant became smaller and smaller. The time came when it consisted (as far as we know) of no more than Zacharias and Elizabeth, Mary and Joseph, Simeon and Anna, and a handful of shepherds. Nobody else in Judea was ready to welcome Abraham's promised Seed into the world. Nobody else recognized the Light who had come to lighten the Gentiles, the Glory of God's people, Israel.

In the days of the Babylonian exile this remnant was represented by Daniel, Hananiah, Mishael and Azariah (Daniel 1:6). Just four candles, and a few more, shone in the godless darkness of those times. Only a handful of lives

Setting the scene

remained true to God. At a time when nobody else cared, God and His Word continued to matter to this small group.

God is not much interested in numbers, but He is insistent that He will never leave Himself without witnesses. True religion continues uninterrupted in the world, but its adherents are seldom numbered in more than handfuls. In Babylon God was content that His true Israel should be whittled down to single figures. The first six chapters of Daniel tell us how this little remnant remained true to God in a hostile environment.

The main lesson

The previous sentence brings us to the main lesson of this book. Daniel tells us how to remain true to God in a hostile environment. It shows us how to live for Him when everything is against us. From its pages we learn how to sing the Lord's song in a strange land. Daniel and his three companions managed it. So can we.

It *is* possible for a person to live for God when there is nothing on his side. Noah, Abraham, Moses and David were all godly men, yet God's Word records that each of them fell, at some time, into a serious fault. Each of them has at least one blemish on his character, and some of them more than one. The Bible does not whitewash its leading characters, or pretend that they were something other than what they really were. But the same book does not record any blemish in the life of Daniel. Spirituality and integrity of character do not require ideal conditions in which to develop. They are not plants that thrive in the protection of the greenhouse, but grow best when exposed to snow, wind and hail, to drought and burning sun.

Think of it! A fourteen-year-old boy (that is all he was) was taken from his home, family and friends, and forcibly marched to a strange land. There he was subjected to a powerful and subtle form of indoctrination, which we shall read about shortly. In later years he was surrounded by jealous enemies who plotted against his life. At no time was he free from the temptation to pursue material prosperity and personal advancement at the expense of everything else. He was surrounded by evil in youth, middle years and old age. There is hardly a temptation known to any of us that he did not have to face. And yet the Scriptures do not record a single blemish in his character! He purposed in his heart to please God, and never moved from that resolve. It *is* possible to live for God in a hostile world. Godliness can, and does thrive where there are no ideal circumstances.

Very few (if any) of us have faced the difficulties that Daniel faced. When we think of difficulties, we usually think only of our own. We persuade ourselves that everyone else has it easy, and that we would make more spiritual progress if we were in some other situation. The factory worker thinks that it is easier to live the Christian life in the office, while the office worker is convinced that it is easier to be a Christian housewife at home. The housewife is not aware of the difficulties of living for Christ at school, and the school student looks forward to the day when he will face the comparatively easier challenge of the factory floor. And so the circle goes on. We each imagine that nobody has difficulties as great as our own. We excuse our poor standard of Christian living by pointing to the circumstances in which we are found. The book of Daniel exposes us completely. It proves that true spirituality never depended upon things being easy.

What was Daniel's secret?

It is simple. Before he interpreted Nebuchadnezzar's dream, what did he do? He prayed (2:17-19). When he was plotted against, and then thrown into a den of lions, what was he doing? He was praying (6:10). What is chapter 9 about? It is Daniel at prayer. He was a man of prayer. A proper prayer life is half the secret of remaining true to God in a hostile world.

The other half of the secret is just as simple. In 9:2 we shall read of Daniel examining 'books' and understanding them. What books were those? They were the prophetical books of the Old Testament that had been written by that date. In 9:11 and 9:13 we shall read of him referring to 'the law of Moses'. Daniel read, and knew his Bible. His secret is easy to define, even if not always easy to implement. He stood firm for God in a hostile world because he read his Bible and said his prayers!

These undramatic disciplines need stressing today. It is often thought that the secret of Christian living lies in our having some new and exceptional experience of God. Different terms are used by different people, but the idea is usually very much the same. It is taught that a new experience of God will lead me on to a higher plane than where I am now living. If I can only have this new experience I will never be the same again. All my energies must be devoted to seeking entry to this higher life, and I must not rest until the new experience that I seek is truly mine.

Daniel had wonderful experiences of the Lord, but he did not seek them. He sought God *for His own sake* and not for what He might do for him. He enjoyed being with Him, discerning His will from His Word, and communing with Him in prayer. We underline it again. His secret was too simple to miss: he read his Bible and said his prayers.

This, too, was the secret of the early Christian martyrs, the persecuted Reformers and their children, and the zealous and evangelizing Methodists. This was the secret of the great pioneering missionaries of the last century. They were well aware that 'the people that do know their God shall be strong, and do exploits' (11:32). Like Daniel, they lived in two worlds. Like Daniel, they often saw *that* world intervening in the affairs of this one. They became God's friends, and 'greatly beloved' (10:19) in heaven. That was their secret!

Knowing this, let us now study the book of Daniel, and learn, in our turn, how to stand alone.

2.
OFF TO BABYLON!

Please read Daniel chapter 1

The first chapter of Daniel, like the last, is very brief. It is a simple and straightforward narrative designed to teach us at the outset a lesson that we must not miss. The chapter divides into four parts.

Nebuchadnezzar's expedition against Jerusalem

The first two verses tell us about Nebuchadnezzar's expedition against Jerusalem. It is important that we remember that we are not reading a fable. We are dealing with history — with events which really took place.

It is 605 B.C. From Babylon comes Nebuchadnezzar, who has just become King of Babylon earlier in the same year. He besieges Jerusalem. He defeats it, enters it and takes off to Babylon just what and whom he likes. However, he does not take the king. Jehoiakim remains as his puppet king for the next eight years. After that he is to rebel, and will be ruined.

But Nebuchadnezzar does take to Babylon a number of captives, and a large part of the temple treasures. The city remains intact, but the temple is spoiled. This was no accident. It was the Lord's doing, as are all historical events. For too long the Jews had trusted in the temple, and not in the Lord whom they claimed to worship there. Despite the warnings of the prophets, they had believed that the very existence of the temple would guarantee them immunity from any threatened invasion. 'As long as we have the temple, we are safe,' they had said. 'Do you think that Jehovah will ever let His temple be destroyed? Of course not! When the temple is threatened He will certainly step in to rescue us.'

Believing this, the nation had continued in its sin. The

idolatry, immorality and injustice had gone on unabated. The lying and stealing increased without restraint. They were sure that, however they lived, the temple would save them. But it had not. It was now in ruins and a pagan king was carrying its treasures into the house of his god, and into his treasury. By these events God demonstrated that He would not tolerate sin, wherever it was found. He would have turned from His anger, had the people turned to *Him*. But trust in His temple was no substitute for repentance.

God rules, whether His temple exists or not. He remains God, whatever happens on earth. Indeed, whatever happens on earth occurs because He *is* God. 'The *Lord* gave Jehoiakim king of Judah into his hand' (2). He is perfectly in control of history and well able to implement His threats. The conquered city, the spoiled temple, the transported treasures and the weeping captives — they were all His doing, and for the furtherance of His purposes. The experience of His people was defeat, ruin and destruction. He remained the undefeated God, working in and through it all.

Daniel and his three companions introduced

It is with this scene before us that verses 3 to 7 now introduce us to the main characters of the book. It comes about like this.

Nebuchadnezzar was brilliant. He was a genius, and far too subtle to fall into the mistake of the Pharaoh who had oppressed the Hebrews in Egypt. You will remember that his approach had been thoroughly crude. He had treated the Hebrews like slaves, crushed them and put them under the jackboot.

There is always a high risk that people treated like that will revolt. This was something that Nebuchadnezzar wanted to avoid at all costs. Babylon was conquering the world. Before long the number of people conquered would be far greater than those who had conquered them. It would be militarily impossible for Babylon to sustain an oppressive regime throughout the known world. There were simply too many people to keep down, and too few soldiers to do it. Another way would have to be found by which the conquered nations could be kept loyal to the empire.

Nebuchadnezzar's method was to take the cream from every nation that he conquered, and to assimilate it into the Babylonian civil service. In this way the various parts of his ever-increasing dominions were ruled by those who would otherwise be captives. Those who rebelled would have to rebel against their own people — perhaps against their own sons.

This was the method that Nebuchadnezzar employed when he conquered Judah, as verse 3 makes clear. He instructed Ashpenaz, 'the master of his eunuchs' (that is, the chief official of his civil service) to take the very best of Judah's youth, and to put them into places of responsibility. They were to enter his personal kingly service and growing administration. They were to walk the corridors of power. Ashpenaz was to look for likely candidates from the royalty and nobility of the Jewish nation.

Some people teach that such young men were then made into eunuchs, but this cannot be so, for verse 4 tells us that they had to be wholly without defect. This verse also tells us that they had to be good-looking, intelligent in every branch of learning, well-informed, and young men who were fit to take their place in the king's personal service. Nebuchadnezzar was to have only the best!

Once selected, these young people were to embark upon a comprehensive programme of re-education where particular importance was to be laid upon a thorough grounding in the language and literature of the Babylonians. Nothing would be permitted to distract them from their studies. In addition to language and literature, the next three years were to be filled with lessons in mathematics, science, navigation, politics, history and geography — in fact the whole spectrum of Babylonian learning was going to be instilled into their young minds. The last thing they were going to need to think about was their food and drink. This would be prepared for them, and served just as if they were members of the royal household (5).

How many students reading these pages have been diverted from their studies because, living in a bed-sit, they have had to shop for their own food and to prepare their own meals? No such danger faced Daniel, Hananiah, Mishael and Azariah. They had nothing but their studies to think about. They were even to forget that they were Jews and were to become Babylonians. They were to forget that they were God's servants, and were to become the servants of an earthly king.

This explains verse 7. It was Babylonian policy that all those selected for re-education and special training should have their names changed. Daniel (which means 'God has judged') became Belteshazzar ('Keeper of the hidden treasures of Bel'). Hananiah ('Jehovah has been gracious') became Shadrach. We do not know what that name means, but it contains the name of the pagan deity Marduk. Mishael ('Who is like God?') became Meshach — a name which contains one of the ancient forms of the name for the deity Venus. Azariah ('Jehovah has helped') became Abed-nego ('the servant of Nebo').

When we look at the four original names we find that two of them end in 'el', which is one of the names of God; and two of them end in 'iah' or 'jah', which is a shorthand version of 'Jehovah'. These names are changed by the Babylonians to names which refer to the pagan deities of Bel, Marduk, Venus and Nebo. The four boys would have been fourteen years old when their names were changed, for this was the age at which the Babylonians entered young people upon their programme of re-education. They were to be given no rest until they had a thorough grasp of all that was required of them. That would be three years later. Stolen from their homes, told to forget their God, intensively re-educated in a pagan culture — how would these young boys fare? Would they remain true to their God, and to what they knew to be right? Or would they capitulate?

Is it possible that they also faced pressure from another source? Could it be that, as they marched off, some of the Jews applauded and said, 'Captivity isn't going to be so bad for them. The king is going to do something for our boys. Our boys are going to *be* somebody'?

Yes, the boys *were* going to be somebody — but at the expense of losing their identity as the children of God. Would they be able to withstand the pressure? And can the Christian today stand firm when the media and society at large bombard his mind day and night, putting him under pressure to change his mind and to think differently? Is it possible for him to remember his privileged status as a child of God, and to live accordingly, when everything around him is telling him to give his mind to *other* things?

Their stand

What happened next is in verses 8 to 16, and to understand these verses we must recall why the Jews were going into captivity at all. The whole nation was at a low level spiritually, and therefore morally too. The crying sin had been idolatry. The exile was a punishment for all of the nation's sins, but for that one in particular, and they were to remain in Babylon until they had finished with it for ever. Whatever mistakes the Jews fell into in the post-exilic period, idolatry was not one of them. The exile cured them for good. But at the time the exile occurred, idolatry was a feature of the national life, and what marked out the godly remnant from all the others was their adamant refusal to have anything to do with it.

Imagine, then, these four boys starting their re-education. They are told that instead of preparing their own food, they are to be fed from the royal table. The reason that they turned down the royal food was not because of the Jewish food laws. They could at least have had the wine, for no Jewish food law ever forbade it. The reason for their refusal was that the food from the king's table had been offered to idols before it was served. Every Babylonian kingly meal began with an act of pagan worship. They were a lot more diligent about this than many Christians are about saying grace before eating. Nothing was eaten and nothing was drunk until it was dedicated to certain pagan deities. Those who ate the food were reckoned to have participated in the pagan rites. It was precisely because they refused to compromise with idolatry that the four boys had a place among the godly remnant. They were certainly not going to have anything to do with it now.

'But, Daniel, aren't you being rather extreme?'

That is how many people would talk today. They would say, 'Why make a fuss about such a small thing as eating food offered to idols? You could lose your head for refusing food from the king's table. Why not put your scruples aside? Just think what influence you can have by being in the civil service in Babylon. Perhaps you could get to the very top. Wouldn't it be marvellous for one of God's children to be in such a position? As it is, you are endangering your very life. Even if you don't lose your head, it seems likely that you will end up in a dungeon. You will certainly never get to the top unless you obey the king's instructions.'

The reply of Daniel, and each of his three companions, is 'No! I will not eat, because I will abstain from every appearance of evil. Although it means great personal danger, and although it might cost me my life, I would rather rot in a dungeon or die by execution than be associated with idolatry. I would rather die than sin even a little.' *That* is the spirit to which we refer when we say, 'Dare to be a Daniel!'

Of course, we must not get the impression that Daniel was unpleasant in the way that he refused the royal food. The language of verse 8 is very careful. 'Daniel purposed in his heart that he would not defile himself with the portion of the king's meat, nor with the wine which he drank: therefore he *requested* of the prince of the eunuchs that he might not defile himself.' He went to the chief official and put his point to him. He remained firm and principled, but was also kind and courteous as he asked to be released from his obligation to eat the food.

The sheer integrity of Daniel had already brought him into favour with the chief official (9), but he, not unnaturally, was a bit worried about his own head. 'Look, Daniel, if you don't turn out like you are supposed to, it is all up with me.'

The measure of Daniel is seen in that he refused to give up. He was not going to be moved. In verses 11 to 14 we see him going to the official below the chief official and saying, 'Just give us ten days trial. For ten days let us eat nothing but pulse.'

'Pulse' certainly sounds very far from appetizing! In fact it was a mixture of fresh vegetables and fresh fruit. Daniel was suggesting a diet of perpetual salad! It did not matter to him how often he had it. Anything would be better than eating food which was associated with the worship of idols.

'Just give us ten days trial, and no wine — we will drink water instead.' Daniel's example is worthy of our serious consideration. He was wise, tactful, kind and sensitive. But he was also firm.

Verses 15 and 16 tell us of the effect of this unvaried diet. The boys in no way suffered by their abstinence from the luxurious foods of the king's table. Even after ten days there was a noticeable improvement in their complexion, and they were equally obviously making good progress physically — and in every way were very much better than those who continued with the prescribed diet.

The lesson is that *nobody* loses out by refusing to compromise. The official's fears were entirely allayed, and he gave permission for the boys to remain permanently on their chosen diet. Nobody had been offended. Yet neither Daniel nor his three companions had compromised. They had been faithful in little, and this was to be the beginning of their being faithful in much.

If Daniel had not stood firm at this point, could he possibly have stood firm later, when threatened with death in a lions' den? If his three companions had compromised in their early life, how would they have fared when faced by a burning fiery furnace? It is because they honoured God in a small thing that they were able to honour Him when bigger issues were at stake. People who fall into serious sins only do so because they have learned to tolerate smaller ones.

The outcome

The immediate outcome of their courageous and spiritual action is recorded in verses 17 to 21. They had put God before every other consideration. He in turn honoured them, and stirred up in their lives gifts which they had never dreamed that they had.

This often happens. I knew a man years ago who was totally illiterate. He could not read so much as a word. When the Lord saved him, he concluded that he could walk with God better if he could read His Word. With considerable perseverance, and at great personal cost, he set about learning to read. In doing so he discovered (to his amazement) that he had really quite a good mind. He became an avid reader, and managed to get a job as a postman. In more recent years he has become a pastor. Since his childhood everybody had said that nothing would become of him. When he put God first, and determined to please Him, he suddenly discovered that he had gifts which neither he, nor anyone else, had ever imagined he possessed.

This is precisely what happened to Daniel, Hananiah, Mishael and Azariah. They put God first, and set themselves to their studies. He blessed them with brilliance.

Has something similar happened in your own experience?

You saw something that needed doing and, for the Lord's sake alone, you set yourself to do it. In doing so, you discovered that you possessed gifts of which you were entirely ignorant previously. You became aware, perhaps, that you had a flair for administration, or that you could communicate easily with young people. Gifts came to light in your life simply because you put God first and, very often, the discovery of these gifts has later put you in good stead in your daily work as well. This experience is in no way appreciably different from what happened in Daniel 1. Daniel, of course, had another gift as well. It is to figure prominently in this book, and receives its first mention in verse 17.

And so, at last, the three-year course ended. It was time for the final exams. As in the British universities of bygone days, these exams were not written, but oral. The students had to appear before the king, who personally examined each one and gave his assessment. His estimate of Daniel, Hananiah, Mishael and Azariah is preserved for us in verses 19 and 20. They were better than all the other students. But that is not all. They were better than even the existing graduates who had finished their studies, and were now occupying leading positions in the empire. In fact they were *ten* times better! As a result each of the four found himself in a high position where he could use his influence for God. The Lord could entrust them with such promotion because they had demonstrated at base level that, come what may, even when in personal danger, they would remain true to Him. Daniel was to remain in such a position for seventy years (21)!

Many believers are yearning for higher positions where they can have more spiritual influence. Teachers long to be heads, juniors look forward to being managers, and union members hope to become shop stewards. 'If only I were there,' they say, 'what influence I could have for the Lord!'

None of us can make a higher position count for God unless we live for Him *now,* where we are. If we are unwilling to stand up and be counted for Him over small things, how will we ever do so over bigger things? Is it possible to be faithful in much without first being faithful in little? If we cannot resist comparatively small temptations, what will we do when they are intensified?

The central lesson of Daniel 1 can be summarized in a single phrase: 'Them that honour me I will honour' (1 Samuel 2:30).

3.
NEBUCHADNEZZAR'S DREAM

Please read Daniel chapter 2

We are, then, in the sixth century before Christ. As a punishment for their sins, and especially for their idolatry, the Jews are captives in Babylon. God has warned them repeatedly, and they have not listened. Yet within the apostate nation there is still a handful true to God, and four of them now occupy important and influential positions in the Babylonian civil service. These four are the chief characters of the book of Daniel, and in this chapter we see how this godly remnant was not only preserved, but actually raised to a position of greater influence in pagan Babylon. It seemed certain that God's true Israel would be obliterated. It appeared certain that the small minority who held to His truth would be destroyed. But God's remnant is the object of His special care, and He rules history to their advantage — as we shall now see.

What Nebuchadnezzar saw

The first thirteen verses of the chapter tell us of three things which King Nebuchadnezzar saw. The first of these was *a dream* which he refused to relate or describe. It was the second year of his reign, and he had gone to bed thinking about the future. He was the linchpin of an immense empire, and it was quite natural that, as the last thought of the day, he should have wondered what the future held (29).

As we know, very often the things which are on our minds during the day, and especially as we go to sleep, are the things that we dream about. But Nebuchadnezzar's dream was not an ordinary dream. It was given by God. Its vividness was particularly intense, and the king was terror-stricken. Often when someone has a nightmare he wakes up with a start, and

Daniel 2

the impression of his dream lingers on. At last, however, it goes away. Not so with Nebuchadnezzar! Agitated in spirit, he has woken up and is quite unable to shake off the dream. His sleep has fled from him, and he lies terrified upon the royal bed.

Immediately he summons the people whom he thinks can interpret his dream and make its meaning plain (2). He has all sorts of 'hangers-on' in his court: there are soothsayers and magicians and astrologers and sorcerers, and a special group of people called the 'Chaldeans', who are not to be confused with the nation which carried the same name. He tells them of his agitation of spirit, and that he wants to know what the dream means (3). The dream is haunting him. He cannot get it out of his mind.

From verse 4 to the end of chapter 7, the book of Daniel is in the Syriac language, better known as Chaldee or Aramaic. The verse records the answer of the king's courtiers to his request. They reply with a request of their own. It is a reasonable request, even though it is phrased somewhat arrogantly. 'King,' they say, 'you tell us the dream, and we will give you the interpretation. Describe what you saw, and we in turn will tell you what it means.'

This apparently reasonable request is met by a blood-curdling threat! Such threats were typical of oriental despots at that time and Nebuchadnezzar, for one, was well able to carry out what he said.

'The thing has gone from me,' he says. This does not mean, as is often imagined, that Nebuchadnezzar had forgotten his dream. If this were so, how could it still be troubling him? If the king could not remember the dream, then the end of verse 9 does not make any sense either. It was because he *did* remember the dream that he could check up whether they had related it accurately, and could therefore also have confidence that their interpretation of it was correct.

When in verse 5 Nebuchadnezzar says, 'The thing has gone from me,' he means, 'The decree has gone from me ... if you will not tell me both what the dream was, and what it means, I will cut you in pieces and tear down your houses. After all, interpreting dreams is your business. It is what you are paid to do' (5).

Also typical of the rulers of the time are the extravagant honours promised in verse 6. Failure to tell the dream and to interpret it would mean certain destruction. But success would mean honour and advancement and reward.

The dream was not the only thing Nebuchadnezzar saw. He also saw *the astrologers playing for time,* as we see in verses 7 to 11. The blood-curdling threat and the extravagant promise quickly cured their arrogance, and in verse 7 we see them addressing the king a little more politely: 'Let the king tell his servants the dream, and we will shew the interpretation of it.'

The king's answer is nothing if not blunt (8-9). 'You are just playing for time, because you are completely unable to do what I have asked of you. You are hoping that I will change my mind about destroying you if you fail to give me the interpretation. Indeed, if you can't even tell me what the dream is, then there is no chance that you can give me an accurate interpretation. If you can't tell me what the dream is, you are demonstrating quite forcefully that you are nothing but counterfeits and charlatans. There can be only one decree for people like that. It is the decree of destruction that I have already spoken about.'

'But,' stammer the astrologers in verse 10, 'what you are asking is beyond human power. Nobody in the history of the world has ever asked such a thing before. Usually we just give the interpretation, but this time we are expected to tell you the dream as well. It is too difficult for mere men to do such a thing. The only ones who can do it are the gods themselves.'

Now Nebuchadnezzar saw *red*! 'For this cause the king was angry and very furious ...' (12).

It must have been a fearful sight! The most powerful man in the world in a rage! He had no patience with their confession of impotence. They had said that they could not do it. They had been making all sorts of proud claims, but now he could see right through them. They had claimed to be able to reveal secrets, but could not so much as tell him the content of a dream which was still terrifying him. If they could not do that, how could they possibly do the deeper and more difficult thing which they claimed — to be able to interpret dreams?

'Execute the lot of them!' said the King of Babylon.

The king's rash command is an indication of how much his dream was worrying him. He had to know what it meant! The dream was robbing him of his peace. He could not get it out of his mind. It was with him moment by moment. It haunted him, and never left him. As a result he was in unspeakable turmoil. He had to know what it meant, and so he had no patience with those who said that they were completely powerless to help him.

'Execute all the wise men.'

The command spelt the end of Daniel, Hananiah, Mishael and Azariah. Not that they were astrologers. They had refused to compromise with anything pagan or idolatrous. But we must remember that they had been educated by the wise men of Babylon, and were therefore, in the broadest sense, included among them. The decree of the impatient king, if implemented, would mean the end of the godly remnant. The only people in the world who held to God's truth would be wiped out. The true Israel of God would be extinguished. They had survived the temptation to compromise in chapter 1, but how could they survive this?

What Daniel saw

We answer our question by looking from verse 14 to the end of the chapter. We have seen three things which Nebuchadnezzar saw. We now consider three things that Daniel saw.

First of all he saw *who God is* (14–23). He had a discreet word with the official in charge of executing the wise men and, as a result, the implementing of the decree was delayed.

Daniel's next step was to go to the king. In verse 16 we see him having a royal audience. 'Give me a time,' he entreated, and I will keep the appointment, and give you the interpretation.'

The king evidently acceded to his request, for Daniel's third step is recorded in verses 17 and 18. He went back to the godly remnant, and the four men of faith engaged in united prayer. Their concern, as they prayed, was not that Daniel should have a great reputation as an interpreter of dreams. They desired mercies from the God of heaven, that they should not perish with the rest of the wise men of Babylon.

Four men in a private house began to pray, undoubtedly using arguments, as do all good men of prayer: 'Lord, we are your remnant. A decree has gone out to execute all Babylon's wise men, and we are included in it. If the decree is implemented your remnant will be gone, and the people of God will have vanished from the earth. The true Israel will be finished. Oh Lord, show mercy to us. Give to us an account of the dream, and an understanding of what it means.'

From what we read in 1:17 we know already that Daniel 'had understanding in all visions and dreams'. It was God's special gift to him. That night, or on another night shortly afterwards, the united prayer of God's people was answered, and Daniel knew both what the king saw and what it meant (19). We are not told at once what it was. But we are told that Daniel's immediate reaction to the revelation was to burst out in praise to God. He had a clear understanding of the dream and its interpretation. But he had an even clearer understanding of the being and attributes of God.

Look at what he says about God in verse 20. God is a gracious God, who is wise and mighty.

It is this God who controls history (21). It is not nature. It is not idols. It is *God*! He exercises His power, not only in heaven, but right here upon the earth. We cannot say that we believe in the sovereignty of God unless we believe that.

Daniel had been given a wisdom superior to all the wise men of Babylon, but notice what he says on this subject (21). If a man has wisdom it is because he receives it from God, from whom all wisdom springs. Daniel is quick to acknowledge that he only understands what he now sees because of the undeserved kindness of God (22–23).

Daniel saw who God is. For ourselves, we have here an intimate glimpse into the heart of a godly man. Such a person is quick to lift up his heart to God and to admire Him. He is aware that all he is in himself, and all that he has, are nothing of any worth. He claims no credit for himself, and insists that to God alone should all words and thoughts of praise be given.

Verses 24 to 45 tell us *what Daniel saw in the night visions.* Having thanked God for answered prayer, he is now ready to approach the king.

In the court of Babylon there was a very strict etiquette for such approaches. No doubt this had been observed in verse 16, but it is not recorded there. But it is mentioned this time, and in verse 25 we see that Daniel is ushered into the presence of the

Daniel 2

king by Arioch, and that Arioch takes to himself all the credit for having discovered a man who can interpret dreams.

'Can you really?' questions the king in verse 26. 'Can you really tell me the dream *and* its interpretation?'

'Men can't do it,' replies Daniel (27-28), 'but there is a God in heaven. There is a God in heaven who reveals secrets. He has revealed to you, King Nebuchadnezzar, what will take place in the latter days.'

As soon as we hear Daniel mention 'the latter days' our hearts are excited. The Bible consistently uses this term to refer to the period from Christ's birth to the end of the world. it is not used to refer to the last hours before Christ's return, as Christians sometimes imagine, but for the whole period of world history beginning at Bethlehem's manger. Nebuchadnezzar's dream is going to tell us something about the period of history in which we are still living!

Daniel continues, 'This dream is God's answer to your bedtime thoughts. You went to bed wondering about the future. God answered you in a dream, and I am able to relate to you both the dream and its interpretation. This is not because I am especially wise or exalted. God has given the interpretation to me simply that it might be known ...'.

Verses 31 to 35 record Daniel describing what the king saw, and brings us to the climax of the chapter.

The king, in his dream, saw an immense statue (31). Being almost totally metallic, it gleamed as the sun shone upon it. Its brightness and size made it a terrifying and intimidating sight.

Looking at the image, the king had seen that it was composed of a number of different materials, all but one of which were metals. The head was made of the best gold (32). The chest and the two arms were of silver. The belly and the thighs were of brass, — that is, of bronze, or perhaps copper. The legs, from the knees downwards, were of iron (33). The toes are not mentioned at this stage, but the feet were part of iron and part of clay.

Strange things happen in dreams, and what happened next was as strange as anything anyone has ever seen. Towards the statue came an insignificant stone. Perhaps it was just like one of the little stones that we find in the road. There is no indication where it came from. It appeared to come from nowhere. The king's dream gave him no details of its origin. He simply noticed that it came, and that it dropped upon the feet of the image (34). At once the whole image collapsed, and was reduced to powder. The wind blew over it, and very soon there was no sign that it had ever been there. What had been so terrifying, and what had appeared so permanent and formidable, was gone.

At this point the little stone began to grow. The small stone became a pebble, and then a boulder. As the astonished king watched, it grew — higher than a house, taller than the tallest building, greater than the hills. In fact it became a great mountain that filled the whole world (35).

'This is the dream; and we will tell the interpretation thereof before the king' (36).

'The head, King Nebuchadnezzar, is *you*! You are a world power. You are a kingdom. You are an empire. You are the head of gold!' (37). We should be careful to notice that Daniel addressed his words personally to the king before him, and in no way gave the impression that he was talking about a revived Babylonian empire, as some have thought.

'The chest and the arms are also an empire, albeit a less powerful one, which will follow you' (39).

'The belly and the thighs are another world power to follow that' (39).

'The legs and the feet are yet another world power, which will in turn follow the third one. This fourth empire will be particularly noted for its power to crush. It will have the strength of iron in it. And yet it will be a composite affair — of iron mixed with clay. Its two elements will ultimately find themselves unable to bond to each other, and it will become a divided kingdom. One of the parts will remain strong, but the other will be brittle, and more easily broken.

'And the little stone? Well, during the period of that fourth world power an event of great significance will take place. "In the days of these kings shall the God of heaven set up a kingdom, which shall never be destroyed: and the kingdom shall not be left to other people, but it shall break in pieces and consume all these kingdoms, and it shall stand for ever (44).

'"Forasmuch as thou sawest that the stone was cut out of the mountain without hands, and that it brake in pieces the iron, the brass, the clay, the silver, and the gold; the great God hath made known to the king what shall come to pass hereafter: and the dream is certain, and the interpretation thereof sure"' (45).

So Daniel saw who God is, and also the dream and its interpretation. The third thing that he saw was something that nobody ever expected in Babylon. We see what it was from verse 46 to the end of the chapter. He saw *the king humbled, the true God glorified and the godly remnant promoted.* Who ever expected to see the most powerful man in the world fall on his face in homage?

But that is precisely what happened. At the same time the king commanded that incense should be burned in Daniel's honour. It has sometimes been thought that Nebuchadnezzar was giving to Daniel worship which should be given to God alone. But this is not what was happening. We can perhaps be helped if we remember a similar incident in the life of Alexander the Great. When he came to Jerusalem, he fell at the feet of the high priest, and was severely reprimanded by one of his aides for doing so.

'You don't do that sort of thing,' he said.

'I do not worship the high priest,' replied Alexander, 'but the God with whose high-priesthood he has been honoured.'

Something similar happened in Nebuchadnezzar's throne room. The king fell at Daniel's feet, not because he worshipped Daniel as God, but because he recognized Daniel as God's spokesman. And so the true God was glorified. Nebuchadnezzar did not yet see that the God of Israel was the only God, but did acknowledge Him as the supreme God. Nobody could possibly have thought, a few hours before, that such a thing could happen. It looked as if the days of God's remnant were certainly numbered. It seemed certain that the godly would be destroyed and that they would vanish for ever. But now Daniel, Shadrach, Meshach and Abed-nego were all promoted.

Daniel was promoted over the province of Babel. He became the chief overseer. Archaeology has not yet been able to make clear to us what this appointment involved, although we have found the title 'the chief overseer', to which he was promoted, among the ancient inscriptions.

The three companions who joined with him in prayer were promoted as under-officers to serve beneath him.

The remnant was now not only safe, but influential. It had

had everything stacked against it, but had not died out. It did not die out in chapter 1 simply because it refused to do a wrong thing. It did not die out in this chapter because it gave itself to united prayer. This is the way that a witness to God is preserved in the world, and we would do well to take these lessons to heart.

What we should see

In this chapter we have noted what Nebuchadnezzar saw and what Daniel saw. What should *we* see? In addition to some lessons we have already referred to, there are three principal things.

First of all we should see that *God's Word is true*. Daniel spoke the words which God gave him, and all that he said would happen *did* happen.

Nebuchadnezzar's world empire was followed by three more. We do not need to guess which empires were being referred to in the dream and its interpretation, because three of them are actually identified in the book of Daniel itself and the identity of the fourth is revealed to us by our Lord Jesus Christ. This point needs underlining at a time when so many contradictory things have been written about the vision of chapter 2. There can be no possible doubt about which world powers are being referred to here.

However, it was not four images that Nebuchadnezzar saw, but only one. This is because in a very real sense all the empires of which Daniel spoke are the same empire. The second took over the first. The third took over the second. The fourth took over the third.

The first had a successor. So did the second and third. The fourth did not have a successor, but in the period of that fourth empire another kingdom arose. The little stone can truly be said to have destroyed all four empires, and not just the last.

Babylon disappeared as a world power when it was conquered by, and incorporated into, Medo-Persia. Medo-Persia in turn was conquered by, and incorporated into, Greece. The mighty empire of Greece was, in its turn, displaced by Rome. The Romans did not assimilate all the borders of the Greek empire into their own, and yet established an empire

Daniel 2

more world-wide and expansive than any that had preceded them. It was in the days of the Roman Empire that *another* empire was established — an empire which is ever growing and never ending.

Let us think a little further about this amazing and predictive vision. Of all the four empires one only was a united whole. That was Babylon, which is therefore spoken of as the head of the image. Medo-Persia never enjoyed the glory of Babylon, and cannot be better described than as silver compared with gold. Although it consisted of one body, it was in fact two arms, just as the dream of the image had predicted. Greece followed. Under Alexander the Great it was an undivided empire, but eventually it split into two legs, based on Syria and Egypt.

In the same way the Roman Empire had two great divisions of east and west (and incidentally, eventually split into ten smaller kingdoms, or toes — a subject which is beyond the scope of this particular chapter). It was in the days of Rome's rule that a Stone without origin came to this world. He was without origin, because He existed before all time. John the Baptist said of Him, 'He that cometh after me is preferred before me: for he was before me' (John 1:15). The eternal Son of God came as the insignificant Babe of Bethlehem, to establish an everlasting kingdom. Today the previous kingdoms lie in the dust. But Christ's kingdom remains and is growing and will last for ever. It will never have a successor. Everything has happened as Daniel said it would.

When God speaks, what He says is true. A chapter like this should renew our confidence in God's Word. We should admire it and rest on it in a way that we have not done before. The chapter should bring us to see afresh that 'the judgements of the Lord are true and righteous altogether' (Psalm 19:9).

But we should see something else. We should see that *history is in God's hands.*

The book of Daniel was written in the sixth century B.C. A wide body of opinion does not believe this, and insists that it must have been written in the second century B.C. Such a theory can be discounted entirely — and once more I refer interested readers to the work of E.J. Young mentioned at the end of this book. He, Robert Dick Wilson and others have shown clearly the impossibility of such a view. The reason that this mistaken view is popular is because many men and women cannot accept the idea of predictive prophecy. They just cannot believe that the Word of God can accurately predict events before they occur. Once you start with that assumption, no amount of reasoning, however well founded, will convince you otherwise. This is the main reason why scholars holding to a sixth century date have not been widely heeded. But those with open minds will find their arguments totally convincing. More important, of course, is the clear statement of our Lord Jesus Christ that Daniel is the author of the book that carries his name (Mark 13:14). Who will dare to say that the perfect Son of God was mistaken?

We can, then, confidently assert that Daniel chapter 2 records history before it took place. How could that be, unless God controls history?

It is not sufficient to say that God merely foresaw what would happen. Could He have done this without having a measure of control over the events that He saw? Could He have foreseen it perfectly without controlling it perfectly? None can infallibly predict what he does not entirely control. Perhaps something might go wrong. Somebody might put a spanner in the works. Somebody might choose in a way for which the predictor had made no allowance. You cannot see the future unless you control the future.

And that is exactly what the Scriptures teach. They tell us that God 'hath made of one blood all nations of men for to dwell on all the face of the earth, and hath determined the times before appointed, and the bounds of their habitation' (Acts 17:26).

Daniel has already told us that it is God who appoints and removes kings (21). God controls history. This is a marvellous thought to me as I write these pages. I do not live in a universe which is out of control. I live in a world where God's purposes are coming to pass, even though many events in it are horrific and terrifying — just as they were in the days of the empires mentioned in this chapter. Everything that is happening is steadily moving forwards and bringing to pass what God has planned. God is still on the throne.

This should bring us to see a third thing. *There is no reason for a Christian to be discouraged.*

Christ, the Stone, has set up a kingdom — a sphere where He reigns. It is not a political kingdom, for He has dogmatically asserted, 'My kingdom is not of this world' (John 18:36). He has explained to us what sort of kingdom it is: 'The kingdom of God is within you' (Luke 17:21). Christ's kingdom is a spiritual kingdom.

All over the world are men and women, young people and boys and girls, in whose hearts Christ reigns. Of all nations He has made a new nation. From people of all races He has made a new race. People of all citizenships have a new citizenship. Barriers between Jews and Gentiles, slaves and free, barbarians and cultured Greeks have all been broken down. The realm of Christ's rule is not measured by visible boundaries on the map. He rules in the heart of those individuals who have been brought into union with Him by the gospel.

Christ established this kingdom with the authority of the God of heaven (44). It began to be set up in the days of the Roman Empire, just as predicted, and will never pass away. He remains the perpetual King in it, and will never have a successor. He Himself is the Almighty God, and so the kingdom will never be conquered. Its citizens will never be stolen from Him, nor will they ever revolt, for every one of them is a willing subject.

It is of this marvellous kingdom that this chapter speaks.

Nothing whatever can prevent the growth of this kingdom, and it is from this fact that we should derive immense encouragement. It has always prevailed against all opposition, and it always will. Christians can be burned alive (as done by Nero), thrown to wild animals in amphitheatres, or exiled to the islands. They can be shut up in dungeons, horribly tortured, or publicly executed at Smithfield. Nothing that is done to them stops their number increasing. The blood of the martyrs proves to be the seed of the church. The kingdom grows, and grows, and grows.

At last it will be a mountain which fills the whole earth. This does not mean, of course, that everyone will be saved. But it does mean that ultimately there will be people of every nation and tongue united in the heavenly ascription of praise to the Lord Jesus Christ: 'Worthy is the Lamb that was slain ...'

(Revelation 5:12).

Christ's kingdom is an everlasting kingdom. The day is coming when He will put down all other authority, rule and power (1 Corinthians 15:24). The only rule which will then be seen will be His. The whole universe will acknowledge His lordship, while His willing subjects will be thrilled to hear, 'Come, ye blessed of my Father, inherit the kingdom prepared for you from the foundation of the world' (Matthew 25:34).

No doubt the Lord's people will always be a remnant — a small minority in proportion to the overall population. But the teaching of this chapter assures us that the remnant will always be there. And it will always be growing, until it extends to the end of the earth.

There is no need for any of us to fear for the future of Christ's cause. God's ark is going along very well, and we do not need to put out our hands to steady it. The future of Christ's kingdom is as secure as the promises of this chapter. His kingdom cannot fail. Soon it will be the only kingdom.

This is why it is worth consecrating all that we have and are to the extension of Christ's kingdom. All our possessions and talents and energy should be devoted to the great work of winning others. We cannot fail. We sow the seed. Not all of it grows; not even most of it. But some of it *always does,* and another life then comes to be lived under the lordship of Christ.

How marvellous to be a member of such a kingdom! How awful, by unbelief and failure to repent, to be eternally outside it!

4.
THE BURNING FIERY FURNACE

Please read Daniel chapter 3

If you found yourself smiling every time you read of 'the princes, the governors, and the captains, the judges, the treasurers, the counsellors, the sheriffs, and all the rulers of the provinces', it is because you were intended to do so. The same is true of 'the cornet, flute, harp, sackbut, psaltery, dulcimer, and all kinds of music'. This chapter is pouring scorn upon the pomp and ceremony of the pagan idolatry that it records. It is derisory.

The previous chapters have told us how a small group of people had continued to live for God in a hostile environment. In the nation of Judah, now being punished for its idolatry, there remained only a handful of people whose hearts were true to God. Tempted to compromise, they had refused to do so. When they were apparently on the brink of being destroyed, God had miraculously preserved them. The chapter that we now have open records another marvellous deliverance, and assures us again that the few who remained true to God were the objects of His special care. It contains enormous encouragements, and some important practical lessons, for every believer who finds himself out of step with the standards and values of the world around him.

One of the mysteries of this chapter is that it does not mention Daniel himself. Nobody knows why, though, of course, there has been plenty of speculation. Where he was at this time, and what he was doing, are not revealed. Instead, it is the turn of his three friends to come to the fore. Shadrach, Meshach and Abed-nego have already been mentioned several times in the book, but it has always been Daniel who has been most prominent, and they have been somewhat overshadowed by him, and in the background. Now we are going to see them in their own right.

Chapter 3 is an uncomplicated record of how three men

courageously defied the order of the most powerful man in the world, rather than displease God. To please Him was more important to them than even their own lives. Their example shows to us what is the essence of godliness. The chapter also records how God stepped in and vindicated their faith.

The main thing about this chapter is not the miraculous deliverance. We have no problems in believing in miracles, do we? Once we see that God is almighty, and once we come to believe that He has raised His Son from the dead, miracles are no longer a problem to us. The powerful deliverance recorded in this chapter fills our hearts with worship to God. But it is not the most important thing for us to notice.

The main thing in the chapter is that three young believers are tempted to do wrong, and refuse. They are prepared to be out of step with everybody else, even if it means a terrible death. 'Compromise' is not a word in their vocabulary. Wrong is wrong, and they will not do it, however great is the peril. They will not tolerate sin, or even hold a dialogue with it. It is to this point that we should give our attention, for it teaches us once more how a testimony to God is kept alive in a pagan world. If we are to be true to God in a hostile environment, we ourselves must go the way of Shadrach, Meshach and Abed-nego.

This chapter brings to mind the old riddle: 'What happens when an irresistible force meets an immovable object?' except that in this case there are *three* immovable objects! We shall look at the irresistible force first, then at the immovable objects. Finally we shall see what happened when the two met.

The irresistible force

The irresistible force is King Nebuchadnezzar, and if we survey verses 1 to 7 it will quickly be plain why we are calling him that. The narrative starts with his erecting an image. Precisely when he did this we do not know, and the chapter does not tell us. Perhaps it was soon after Daniel had described him as a 'head of gold'. Possibly the reference had filled him with pride and he had followed the dream of an immense image with an actual one.

It was common among Babylonian and Syrian potentates to erect images in their own honour and what Nebuchadnezzar did would not have been considered particularly unusual. The image was almost certainly of himself. It is equally certain that he was thinking not only of his own honour, but also of the honour of the gods whom he worshipped.

The expense of making and erecting such an image must have been exorbitant. Gold-plated, it stood on its pedestal and was over ninety feet tall, but its width was just nine feet. These proportions are rather grotesque, but are typical of Babylonian statues. We need not conclude that Nebuchadnezzar himself was both unusually tall and pathetically thin! This immense and ugly image was then set up on the plain of Dura.

The Aramaic word which is here translated 'plain' means a flat stretch of land between mountains. The image was set up in a sort of natural arena. Around it were acres of perfectly flat land with mountains ascending on each side. It could probably be seen from dozens of miles away, especially when its gold plate reflected the sun.

When the image was ready there was, in keeping with Babylonian custom, a dedication service. It is this that is referred to in verses 2 and 3. Important officials came from the farthest corners of the Babylonian Empire, and their various ranks are set before us. Probably no one in the known world had ever seen a celebration like it. The crowd would have been immense and the whole pageant would have been infinitely more splendid than the most extravagant coronation. It was an image erected by the mighty Emperor of Babylon, in honour of both himself and his gods, and people would have come from throughout his territories to see it.

In verse 4 we have an understatement. In front of this unprecedented crowd, 'an herald cried aloud'. What a voice he must have had! To the hushed multitude he gives a decree in the name of the king. Nobody is exempt from its demands. Present are different peoples and nations and languages, from all over the Babylonian empire, and what is commanded applies to them all.

Also present at the ceremony is an orchestra, the instruments of which are listed in verses 5, 7, 10 and 15. 'All kinds of music' is a Persian phrase and suggests that the orchestra contained some Persian instruments. This is not surprising, for Persia was a near neighbour. The 'cornet' and 'flute' were Semitic, and suggest that some of the musicians were exiled Jews. The 'harp', 'sackbut' and 'psaltery' were Greek instruments. Babylon had by this time been trading with Greece for over a century, and had evidently also seen fit to incorporate Greek music into its own idiom. The herald's decree is that whenever this orchestra plays, everybody, whoever and wherever they may be, is to fall down and worship the newly erected image.

If verse 6 seems to us to be perplexing and unreasonable, there is something that we should remember. This grotesque statue had been erected in honour of the king and his gods. Not to bow down to it could therefore only be interpreted as an act of disloyalty. It was failure to submit to the word of the king. It was treason. Such misbehaviour could only be rewarded by the horrific death of being thrown into a burning and fiery furnace.

To bow down to such an idol presented no problem to the vast majority of people in the Babylonian Empire, even if they came from conquered nations. All they had to do was to think, 'The gods of Babylon are obviously stronger than our own, otherwise we would not have been defeated. We may as well acknowledge it.'

Even to the Jews in exile such bowing down was not a problem. For generations they had disobeyed God and engaged in idolatry. The stern words of the prophets about the evil of such a practice had been deliberately and continuously ignored. They would have had no qualms of conscience about prostrating themselves before the golden image. Idolatry was now in their bloodstream. Why sentence themselves to certain death by refusing to do something that they had been doing for years?

Universal submission to the king's edict could be expected, for no one was either embarrassed or hurt by it. Nobody, that is, except the godly remnant. The mark of their remaining true to God had been that they had had nothing to do with the worship of false gods. The first commandment was of paramount importance to them. They considered that nothing was more important than loving the Lord their God with all their heart and soul and mind and strength. They had refused to countenance even the eating of food offered to idols, so they were certainly not going to *bow* to one. Everyone else may well submit to the king's decree, but not they. There is a higher Power who has to be obeyed. They alone will be nonconformists. They alone will be different. Wrong is wrong, and it cannot be done, even if the consequence of abstaining is certain death in a burning fiery furnace. When everybody else bows down, they are going to remain standing!

For twenty centuries totalitarian regimes have told Christians that they must either conform to ungodly demands, or die. Never has this been more true than in the present century. In many countries of today's world the Lord's people are suffering persecution. They are languishing in prison, are restricted to the most menial tasks in society, endure the heartbreak of having their children taken from them, scream under torture and die horrible deaths — rather than conform to the demands of authorities who command them to finish with godly disciplines and to give them the place in their lives which should be given to God alone.

Many of us do not live under such regimes. Yet the words of Samuel Rutherford remain true for us, too: 'You will not get leave to steal quietly to heaven in Christ's company without a conflict and a cross.' People around us pressurize us to join them in their sins, saying repeatedly, 'Everybody else does it, so why not you? Why be different? Come on, just once; just this time.'

Young Christians are urged to get drunk with their friends, or to lose their virginity before marriage. The pressure is put on them to lie, to steal, to read dirty books and to watch filthy television programmes and films. The profaning of the sabbath day, the wasting of money, bad time-keeping, gambling, the dishonest acquisition of wealth, and a thousand other sins and indecencies are extolled as virtues. It is the 'in' thing to stand under flashing lights and to 'let yourself go' to sleezy lyrics.

The world has its own fiery furnace waiting for those who do not conform to the worship of its idols. It is the furnace of being sneered at, ridiculed, scorned, ostracized and ignored. Clean-living and God-fearing people are told that they are narrow-minded fuddy-duddies, and are cold-shouldered, being shut out of the lives and affections of those around them. To many young believers the pressure seems irresistible. They feel forced into a choice. They must either give in and be like everybody else; or they must stand out, and lose everything.

That was the choice given to Shadrach, Meshach and Abed-nego!

Three immovable objects

With this straightforward choice before them, what did these three young men do? Verses 8 to 18 tell us.

Their choice was to please God, whatever the consequences. From that position they did not move so much as an inch. The irresistible force of a king's decree met three immovable objects!

Let us try to imagine the scene recorded in verses 8 to 12. Let us try to picture the immense crowd, the excitement and the air of expectancy. At last the orchestra plays and, as commanded, the multitude bows to the earth. There — as conspicuous as can be — are just three people still standing up!

No doubt we have all been to church services where someone remains standing after everybody else has sat down. Nobody fails to notice them. Every eye turns towards them. How much more conspicuous would have been Shadrach, Meshach and Abed-nego! The whole empire is bowing down, but three, and three alone, have the audacity to remain on their feet!

In the light of chapter 1 it was probably widely known that these three did not countenance idolatry. But this time it appears that it is going to ruin them. They are reported by name to the king. Undoubtedly plenty of good things could have been said about them to balance such a report. But nothing of the sort is said. It is roundly declared that these three prominent officials have no regard for the emperor.

Verses 13 to 15 tell us how the king in his fury commanded that the three should be brought at once to him.

'Is it true?' he asks them. He then assures them, just as the world around does to us, that, if it is true, it is not yet too late to change things and to become like everybody else: 'Now if ye be ready that at what time ye hear the sound of the cornet, flute, harp, sackbut, psaltery, and dulcimer, and all kinds of music, ye fall down and worship the image which I have made; well: but if ye worship not, ye shall be cast the same hour into the midst of a burning fiery furnace; and who is that God that shall deliver you out of my hands?' (15).

The world around is very anxious to persuade Christians to conform. It cannot tolerate the conspicuousness of those who do not, and before it attempts to ruin them it tries to persuade them to be the same as everybody else. There is something built

Daniel 3

into the world which makes it very anxious to see the Lord's people conform. It is perplexed and troubled by those who will not bow down to the things to which it bows down. It cannot understand those who have different values. It is particularly disgruntled by those who worship and love the invisible God before anything or anyone else. It would sooner persuade than punish them, but if it cannot persuade them it most certainly *will* punish them. In fact, the threat of punishment is part of its argument in persuasion.

Nebuchadnezzar is more angry in this chapter than he was in the last. How dare they refuse to recognize him as supreme? If they would not acknowledge his supremacy this way, they must do so another way. The fiery furnace would demonstrate where real power lay. Once he, the king, had thrown them in, who was the God who would be able to deliver them?

This is the man who so recently had recognized the power and supremacy of God (2:47)! In his anger the lessons of the recent past have been forgotten. When a person gives way to anger, his better judgement flees from him. He is also far more likely to employ threats than reason.

Verse 16 shows to us why it is right to refer to Shadrach, Meshach and Abed-nego as 'immovable objects'. They 'answered and said to the king, O Nebuchadnezzar, we are not careful to answer thee in this matter'.

What that means is 'Yes, the charges have been made and they are true. We have no defence to make, no apologies and no excuses. The facts are facts and we acknowledge them. It is perfectly true that we have not prostrated ourselves before the golden image. If you throw us into the fiery furnace, so be it. Our God can deliver us. Indeed, He will. But if, in His sovereign pleasure, He chooses *not* to, we *still* will not do the sinful thing which you are commanding' (16-18).

That is faith speaking! It is easy to refuse to bow down if rescue is certain. These three men were confident of rescue. But their determination was that even if they were *not* rescued they would still not bow down. That is how godly faith speaks.

There is a great principle in the Christian life which we do well to remember. In the words of C.H. Spurgeon, 'Your duty is to do the right: consequences are with God... It is yours and mine to do the right though the heavens fall, and follow the command of Christ whatever the consequences may be... O sirs, what have we to do with consequences? Let the heavens fall, but let the good man be obedient to his Master, and loyal to his truth. O man of God, be just and fear not! The consequences are with God, and not with thee.'

This biblical principle is exemplified in Shadrach, Meshach and Abed-nego. Our duty, and the limit of our duty, is to do what is right. That is it. There is nothing more. If doing right means that we are ruined, that is God's affair. Consquences are in His hands, but duty is in ours. Our job in life is to do what pleases Him, whatever the cost, and whatever the outcome.

Shadrach, Meshach and Abed-nego lived by that principle. Never before, as far as we know, had they willingly displeased the king of Babylon. There is no indication that it was something that they wanted. But when the choice is between pleasing the most powerful man on earth and the eternal God, there is only one way to go. The worst the world can do is to kill us.

That is an overwhelmingly comforting thought! All of us are going to die, sooner or later, and are to face God. Surely it is better to be killed prematurely and to face Him in peace, than to live a little longer and to face Him in terror. We know that the grave is not the end. Why then should the mere threat of death be a reason for no longer pleasing Him to whom we shall answer after death? How much less should the weak threat of being sneered at distract us from following our Lord in this world?

Too few believers engage in the sort of holy logic we have just considered, and this explains why so many of them yield to the pressures of the age. They consider the short-term consequences of displeasing the world, and decide what to do in the light of them. Shadrach, Meshach and Abed-nego did exactly the opposite. Whatever may be the consequences, right is right and wrong is wrong. They therefore resolved to do the right, and to leave the outcome with God. It is *that* sort of reasoning which keeps a testimony to God alive in the world. When we abandon it we lose all our power to make an impression for God on those around us.

The irresistible force has met three immovable objects. The most powerful force in the world has commanded, 'Do this!' It has been met by the answer which evil most fears: 'No!' Nebuchadnezzar will not budge from the path he has chosen.

Daniel 3

Shadrach, Meshach and Abed-nego will not budge from the stand they have taken. Whatever will be the outcome? Verses 19 to 30 tell us.

What happened

The outcome was that the three uncomprising believers were thrown into the fire. In the fire they received deliverance. We need to notice that they received deliverance *in* the fire, and not *from* the fire.

The intensity of Nebuchadnezzar's anger even changed his appearance (19)! In his fury he commands that the furnace is to be made seven times hotter than normal. When the godly refuse to compromise there are no limits to the anger of the wicked. Those who say that they are prepared to go into the furnace for the Lord's sake must be brought to realize that that furnace may be considerably hotter than they could possibly have imagined.

It is obvious from verse 20 that Nebuchadnezzar expected opposition to his command to execute the three dissidents, because he put the work into the hands of the strongest men in his army. Verses 21 to 23 see them carrying the three young men, bound in their court clothes, to the top of the furnace.

The furnace was like a great pot. At the bottom, in the side, was a door through which it was stoked. But the top was open. It is to this position that God's faithful remnant is taken. The furnace is so hot that Nebuchadnezzar's aides who carry them there are killed by the intense heat. But not before Shadrach, Meshach and Abed-nego have been thrown in. Those looking in through the stoke-hole see them falling through the flames to the bottom of the furnace. They are bound and helpless and the fire, which has already killed those outside it, is certain to kill them too. It is obviously the end of the people of God.

That is a foolish thing to say!

It is *never* the end of the people of God! The world will never see the disappearance of the faithful remnant. Their number may be small, but they will never cease to exist. Never!

The book of Revelation indicates that this world will see the end of the Christian church as an organized institution. The time will come when people will look for churches in the sense that they have always seen them, but will be unable to find them. But that is not the same as saying that the Christian church itself will be gone. The people of God will be here upon earth right up to the moment of our Lord's coming.

Consider Albania today. You cannot find there any visible sign of the Christian church. There is no visible indication that the Christian church has ever been an influence in the nation. No book in any library carries God's name, except in contempt, and there is not so much as a single cross in any cemetery. And yet there are still many Christ-loving believers in that land. The systematic purges have failed in their attempt to eradicate them. You can never get rid of God's remnant.

Nebuchadnezzar and his courtiers fully expected to hear a few brief shrieks, and to see three corpses burst into flames. That, they thought, would be the end of the matter. There would be no dissidents left. Every living person in Babylonia would be someone willing to bow to Nebuchadnezzar's image.

But, like all evil people who have plotted against God's people, Nebuchadnezzar did not see what he wanted to see. Instead he saw something which caused him to leap from his seat to check with his advisors!

'How many men were thrown into the furnace?'

'Three.'

'In what condition?'

'Bound.'

'Then how is it that I now see four men walking in the flames, with no signs of any bonds? And how is it that the fourth has a supernatural appearance?'

No doubt Nebuchadnezzar described the fourth person in the fire in the terms allowed him by his own religious framework. He called him 'a son of the gods'. Equally clearly there is no doubt that fourth Person is who the Authorized Version says He is — 'the Son of God' (25).

The Bible is quite clear that the Son of God appeared on earth in human form many times before He ever came among us in human flesh. Often in these pre-incarnate theophanies He is described as 'the angel of the Lord' or 'the Angel' (Genesis 48:16). We are not surprised therefore to hear Him referred to as 'his angel' in verse 28 of the present chapter. The Lord Jesus Christ walked in the flames with Shadrach, Meshach and Abed-nego! A promise recently given to God's Israel through the lips of Isaiah proved true: 'When thou passest through the waters, I will be with thee; and through the rivers, they shall not overflow thee: when thou walkest through the fire, thou shalt not be burned; neither shall the flame kindle upon thee' (Isaiah 43:2).

If the three had compromised, they would never have had this privilege of walking with Christ in the furnace's flames. Their fellowship with God would have been broken, and they would have been for ever bound — not with ropes and chains, but with an all-pervading sense of failure, disappointment and uselessness.

Instead, six centuries before His birth as a man, they had the privilege of walking with the second Person of the Trinity, the Son of God. By refusing to sin they had an experience of fellowship with the Lord Jesus Christ which is almost unique in the pages of the Old Testament. Who would ever have believed that such a thing was possible on this earth? If they had tried to save their lives, they truly would have lost them. Life would have been an existence without meaning and without fellowship. But by being willing to lose their lives, they had found them. Nobody loses out by refusing to sin, whatever may be said to the contrary. Deliverance from the fire was never their experience. Deliverance *in* the fire is God's way.

God gives a million consolations to those of His children who refuse to compromise. How much impression would these three have made on the ungodly if they had bowed like all the rest? None whatever! But now here are the ungodly gazing and gaping with amazement through the aperture in the furnace's side. They were witnesses of the dissidents' walk with Christ in the flames, and of their being entirely unharmed. As far as we know, no one was converted that day. But they were to receive an impression of God which would never leave them throughout their lives.

At the end of that momentous day the talk was all about the God of Shadrach, Meshach and Abed-nego. Not a mention more of the hideous image! Out of the fire, at Nebuchadnezzar's request, come the three believers, with not so much as a hair of their heads singed! Nor are their clothes affected, and there is not even a smell of fire upon them!

What a God! His servants completely unharmed! What a great God! Nebuchadnezzar is not yet converted, but the events of the day are too much for him. Once more he is driven to an open recognition of God.

As I write these pages I am sitting in a study in Liverpool, England. The day was when even the unconverted of this nation had a recognition of God. By and large the men and women were without saving faith, and yet God was acknowledged throughout the nation's life. Tens of thousands of even unconverted people went regularly to places of worship, said grace at meals and kept quiet on the sabbath day. They refused to swear, to lie and to get drunk, and opposed those who attempted to undermine family life, gambled and engaged in any form of dishonesty. This was not because they were saved men and women, but because strong impressions of God had been made upon their consciences. The morality of the nation was closely linked to its sense of God.

Our nation is no longer like that and is, in fact, departing further from that position by the minute. The decline started when the church began to compromise. The more it has tried to be trendy and 'with it', the less influence for God has been made upon the people. When the churches began to water down their message, so that they no longer preached anything that was offensive — such as hell and miracles — that was the moment when they lost their power.

It is only when the people of God say, 'No!' to what displeases Him, however distasteful this may be to others, that they make a powerful impression for God upon the wicked.

Look at what Nebuchadnezzar was brought to recognize. From verse 28 we see that he recognized who God *is*. He came to see that God has servants, that God had sent His angel, that God was more powerful than himself, albeit he was the most powerful man in the world, and that God is greater than any other god, and is fit to be worshipped. He did not arrive at the full recognition that God is the *only* God. Nor did he yet come to faith in Christ. Yet certain truths were indelibly burned upon this man's heart.

His reaction was to make the decree of verse 29. There is no way that we can condone or approve what he now commanded. We must remember that he was still an unconverted man, and it has been typical of such men through the ages to try and bring others to some sort of faith by the power of the sword. Men do not come to faith that way, but only men of faith themselves have the spiritual discernment to realize it. Nebuchadnezzar had not yet got that far. So it was that he ordered that whoever should speak ill of the God of Shadrach, Meshach and Abed-nego should be cut in pieces, and his house reduced to a dunghill. From his decree we entirely disassociate ourselves. But we take note of the fact that a powerful impression had been made for God, the godly had been wonderfully preserved by God's gracious power, and a testimony to God continued in that pagan empire.

The continuation of a true witness to God in this world depends upon a single word. Equally, the whole power of the Lord's people to be an effective witness to those around them can be ruined by a single word.

The ruining word is 'Yes'. When the ungodly point to sin, and those who worship God agree to do it, they become like everybody else. In this way they lose all their power to do any good, or to preserve the truth.

When temptations to sin are met by a firm 'No!' the situation is entirely different. For a start, a fiery furnace is certain. You either have to be out of the furnace with Nebuchadnezzar, or in it with Christ. There is no middle way. But the place of unprecedented heat is also the place of unprecedented fellowship with the Saviour. Those who walk there also enjoy the assurance that they are making an indelible mark for God upon unconverted consciences.

There is no fiery furnace which a man can invent that can destroy the people of God. Such furnaces, in fact, turn out to be the very means which God uses to *preserve* His remnant and to keep His truth alive in the world.

5.
NEBUCHADNEZZAR'S TURN

Please read Daniel chapter 4

In chapter 4 of Daniel it is the turn of King Nebuchadnezzar himself to come to the forefront. The chapter records a great turn that took place in his life. It is for these two reasons that we call it 'Nebuchadnezzar's turn'.

Nebuchadnezzar before the events of chapter 4

Let us begin by calling to mind what we have already read about King Nebuchadnezzar. In chapter 1 we learned of his brilliant policy of assimilating Jewish captives into his civil service, with a view to placing them in leading positions in his empire.

We saw how four of those who were selected for the requisite re-education refused to eat the food which the king had prescribed for them, because it had previously been offered to idols. The outcome was that God honoured them for the way that they had honoured Him. These four proved to be better than all their fellow students, and even better than their professors! 'And the king communed with them; and among them all was found none like Daniel, Hananiah, Mishael, and Azariah: therefore stood they before the king' (1:19).

He met men such as he had never met before! Four lads, aged only seventeen, were wiser than his senior counsellors. These same four young men were marked out by the fact that they feared Jehovah. This must have made a deep impression on the mind of Nebuchadnezzar.

But contact with believers, in and of itself, does not convert anybody. This is true even if the believers concerned are quite exceptional, as were these four. The events of chapter 2 make this clear. Nebuchadnezzar was still so obviously a pagan. We

Daniel 4

see him there in the worst possible light — troubled, angry and without compassion. His fury with the wise men who can neither tell nor interpret his dream leads him rashly to order the execution of his wise men throughout his realm. Only a godless man could behave like that.

Daniel, giving all the credit to God, interpreted the dream. He shows how one earthly kingdom will give way to another, and how that in the time of the fourth great world empire there will be set up a kingdom which will never pass away. What the pagan counsellors could never see is revealed to godly Daniel, in response to the united prayer of God's remnant. Nebuchadnezzar is brought to see the bankruptcy of his own religion, and to make the confession of 2:47.

That verse underlines how much the king had been impressed. He is brought to the acknowledgement that Jehovah exists. He is several steps further from total unbelief. He confesses that Jehovah is a true God, who is the greatest God of all, although he has not yet reached the point where he admits that He is the only God.

But the human mind forgets so soon. Very often something which appears immensely important to us has no place in our minds shortly afterwards. This is why the man who, at the end of chapter 2, had some profound sense of God, does not appear to have any at all as chapter 3 opens.

The Nebuchadnezzar of chapter 3 is a monarch who erects a hideous statue and commands that it should be worshipped. Where now is his strong conviction that God is the greatest God of all? He is acting in direct contradiction to the truths that he so recently confessed. The words of his mouth have not touched his heart. His will is not submissive to them.

We must not think that Nebuchadnezzar's action is particularly unusual. There are many people like that. They hear gospel truth. It makes a profound impression on them. It grips and excites them. They are alarmed by what they hear. But there is something inside them which does not want those things to be true. Very often they dig in their heels, and try to live as if the truth they have recently admitted simply cannot be true. They give no place to it in their lives.

Imagine a person who goes away on holiday, and finds that the house he has hired is next to an industrial steam-hammer which functions twenty-four hours a day! During the first night of his holidays he cannot sleep a wink. He has never heard a sound like it. It is a repetitive thunder which actually shakes the bed on which he is lying!

The next night he hears the same noise. It is no different in any detail. Yet he finds that he is able to doze off for at least a few minutes here and there. Within a week he is sleeping most of the night, and before his holiday ends he sleeps as soundly as those who have lived in that village all their lives. What so profoundly alarmed him no longer makes any impression. It is as if there were no noise at all. It has no effect on him.

That is often the experience of men and women who are exposed to the things of God. When they first hear them they are alarmed, but come eventually to the place where they are entirely unaffected by what they hear. They are no nearer to bowing the knee to God than they were at the beginning.

That was Nebuchadnezzar's condition in chapter 3, and God really had to shake him up. His unconverted fury led him to throw the three dissidents into the burning fiery furnace, but their miraculous deliverance, coupled with his own sight of the Son of God, moved him to make the confession of 3:28-29. His previous recognition of Jehovah as the greatest God is now even clearer. He admits that no other God can deliver like He can. He is almost on the verge of saying that there *is* no other God.

Yet there is not the slightest hint in the narrative that his own will has been broken. There is no indication that he has yet come to the point of bowing to God and worshipping Him. In his heart of hearts he remains as stubborn as before.

To use the language of our forefathers, he has both *notitia* and *assensus,* but not *fiducia.* In other words, he has heard the truth and taken note of it, and assents to the fact that it is true. But he does not commit himself to what he thus knows to be true. He does not rest upon it, and make it the basis of his trust.

The story of Nebuchadnezzar brings us to see how longsuffering God is. He has spoken to him indirectly in chapter 1. He has spoken to him directly in chapter 2. He has actually shaken him in chapter 3. God has knocked, and knocked, and knocked again. But the heart of the king is not yet open to God. In chapter 4 He is going to knock once more. God's grace is a sovereign grace, and this time He is going to knock in such a way that the door will come right off its hinges.

Daniel 4

God has determined to enter Nebuchadnezzar's heart, so enter it He will!

Nebuchadnezzar after the events of chapter 4

Obviously chapter 4 was written after the events which it records, and by looking at its beginning and end we can see how what happened changed Nebuchadnezzar profoundly.

The chapter opens in verses 1 to 3 with a proclamation. In a manner typical of Babylonian kings, Nebuchadnezzar announces himself as the king of the known world. But verse 2 arrests us. Here he plainly declares that God has worked in his life. The Hebrew word here translated 'sign' means a miraculous event. The word 'wonder' means an event with wonderful effects. Nebuchadnezzar is here saying to his readers, 'God has worked in my life. He has done a miraculous thing, and it has had wonderful effects.'

Verse 3 is no less arresting. It extols the greatness of the miracles which God works and applauds the remarkable effects that they have in people's lives. But there is a new and strange humility in the sentence which follows. We detect a sense of reverent worship in the man's words: 'His kingdom is an everlasting kingdom, and his dominion is from generation to generation.'

We were aware that the king knew the truth (*notitia*). We were aware that he had come to acknowledge it as truth (*assensus*). But now he appears to be bowing to the God of heaven (*fiducia*). He is no longer talking about Him in comparison with other gods. His words do not admit that there are any others.

A great change has come over Nebuchadnezzar, and it is emphasized even more by studying the end of the chapter.

Verse 34 contains the following acknowledgement: 'I Nebuchadnezzar lifted up mine eyes unto heaven, and mine understanding returned unto me, and I blessed the most High, and I praised and honoured him that liveth for ever, whose dominion is an everlasting dominion, and his kingdom is from generation to generation.'

But there is more to come! Verse 35 is also the words of Nebuchadnezzar, and contains the most comprehensive statement of the sovereignty of God to be found anywhere in the Old Testament: 'And all the inhabitants of the earth are reputed as nothing: and he doeth according to his will in the army of heaven, and among the inhabitants of the earth: and none can stay his hand, or say unto him, What doest thou?'

Even that is not the end. The closing verse of the chapter contains Nebuchadnezzar's personal confession of faith: 'Now I Nebuchadnezzar praise and extol and honour the King of heaven, all whose works are truth, and his ways judgement (or justice): and those that walk in pride he is able to abase.'

Chapter 4 of Daniel closes with a worshipping king. We see a man prostrate before God, recognizing Him as both true and just. In his worship there is evidence both of enthusiasm and humility. His faith may have been very weak, but it was *real*. His knowledge may have been meagre, but it was a true knowledge. The important fact is that the king is a changed man. He is different. He has been turned round. He has been converted!

Thank God that there *is* such a thing as conversion! He who was once one thing is now another. There is now spiritual life in the king's heart. But what are the events which turned him from what he once was to what he now is? What was it that brought about Nebuchadnezzar's turn?

The events of chapter 4 — the conversion of Nebuchadnezzar

It is outside the scope of this book to examine every detail of the narrative which is before us. Instead we are going to focus on two points of particular importance.

The first point that we notice about Nebuchadnezzar's conversion is that God did it. *God did it!*

In verses 4 and 5 we learn that when everything was going well with him God intervened and gave him a terrible dream. Once more Nebuchadnezzar sends for those who are supposed to be able to interpret dreams, and once more they are unable to help him.

Considering his previous experience, why on earth did he not ask Daniel to come right away?

The answer is that Nebuchadnezzar had a shrewd idea of what the dream was about, and hoped against hope that it was

Daniel 4

not true. For this reason he did not send for the person whom he knew in his heart would tell him what he did not want to know.

In Babylonian literature it is common to represent a king as a tree. Nebuchadnezzar knew very well that the tree in his dream was himself, and the animals underneath it and the birds in its foliage were the citizens living under his authority and protection. When he saw the tree chopped down, he knew that he himself was going to be humbled and humiliated. From verse 17 it is plain that he must have understood that it was God who was going to do this to him. In his unconverted state it was a truth which he could not face. It was a truth which he did not want to hear.

So he sends for all his pagan interpreters, nursing the hope that they will come up with a different interpretation from the one which his conscience knows to be true, and which he knew Daniel would give to him if he were present. He simply does not want to hear that God is going to lay him in the dust. But when nobody comes up with any sort of interpretation, he is forced into the position of sending for Daniel, and hearing from God's prophet the very truth he has done his utmost to avoid.

Verses 10 to 16 tell us about the dream. There is a tree ... and it is growing ... and growing ... and growing. It appears to reach to heaven and wherever you are, and however far off, you can see it.

An angel descends who demands that the tree should be cut down. Its branches are to be cut off, its leaves stripped and its fruit scattered. The animals and birds will no longer enjoy its shelter. The beautiful tree is to be destroyed. Nothing is to be left but a bare stump, bound around with a metal band.

The stump is as nothing compared with the original tree. It is to stay out in the field, with the beasts which graze there and with the dew forming upon it. The tree's reason is to be taken from it (16) and it is to be given the heart of a beast. It is to stay like this for 'seven times', which means seven definite periods, but whether these are months or years we do not know. All this is to happen at the decree of angels.

In verses 19 to 27 Daniel, with his God-given ability to interpret dreams, unveils its meaning.

He wishes well to the king, and is amazed at the weighty judgements from God which are about to fall on him.

Reluctant to announce the interpretation, he obeys the king's charge to do so.

'King Nebuchadnezzar, you are the tree. You are growing and you are becoming mighty, but you are going to be cut down. This does not happen by the decree of angels, but by the decree of God, whose servants the angels are' (24).

And the purpose of all this? The end of verse 25 tells us. '... Till thou know that the most High ruleth in the kingdom of men, and giveth it to whomsoever he will.'

'But,' continues Daniel, 'you are not going to lose your kingdom entirely. When all this has happened to you, it is going to be restored to you. So repent! Such repentance will not stop the dream happening, but it will lengthen the period of your tranquillity' (27).

'All this came upon the king Nebuchadnezzar' (28). The dream, as it had been interpreted and applied by Daniel, was fulfilled in all its details. This fulfilment is recorded for us in verses 28 to 33.

The moment of the King's humiliation was the moment of his highest pride. It occurred as he surveyed his capital while walking on his palace roof, and said to himself, 'Is not this great Babylon, that I have built for the house of the kingdom by the might of my power, and for the honour of my majesty?' (30). Twelve months had elapsed since his humiliation had been predicted. Perhaps he had come to think that it would not now happen. But God's purpose proceeds exactly as His Word has declared, even if human calendars consider that it is suffering from delay.

We know from history and from archaeology that Nebuchadnezzar was a great builder. All over his dominions were great temples erected under his patronage, as well as scores of wonderful civic buildings in his capital. Included among his achievements were the famous Hanging Gardens of Babylon, which for a long time were numbered among the seven wonders of the world. Babylon was a beautiful place. The king's accomplishments were little short of amazing. His heart was filled with self-admiration. 'I've done it. It took great power to bring all this about, and it was I who wielded that power. Was there ever majesty like mine?'

It was a man whose heart was filled with pride that God struck down. An audible voice from heaven announced that

Daniel 4

the long promised doom had now come (31-32). 'They shall drive thee from men, and thy dwelling shall be with the beasts of the field: they shall make thee to eat grass as oxen, and seven times shall pass over thee, until thou know that the most High ruleth in the kingdom of men, and giveth it to whomsoever he will.'

And it happened! 'The same hour was the thing fulfilled upon Nebuchadnezzar: and he was driven from men, and did eat grass as oxen, and his body was wet with the dew of heaven, till his hairs were grown like eagles' feathers, and his nails like birds' claws' (33).

The great king of Babylon became quite mad. God took away his reason and gave him the mind of a beast. His hair grew until its matted strands looked like feathers. His uncut nails soon resembled claws. Out in the field he lived like an animal, eating grass and being soaked with the morning dew, just like the oxen that surrounded him.

Pagan writers of the ancient world tell us that after fighting his great wars and returning to Babylon, Nebuchadnezzar suddenly disappeared and emerged only a short while before his death. They tell us that one day he was seen on the roof of his palace, from where he had a vantage point from which he could survey his whole city. That was the last that was seen of him for a very considerable period, until just before his death.

Other ancient pagan writers say that he was seized by some form of divinity, while others comment that he was afflicted by a strange illness.

God struck the proud king with an affliction known as 'lycanthropy'. This is where a person thinks himself to be an animal while, at the same time, preserving sufficient inner consciousness to remember who he actually is. People suffering from this dreadful complaint act like the animal they imagine themselves to be, and make whatever noises characterize it.

One particular form of this disease is called 'boanthropy'. Many examples of it have been recorded, and there were a surprisingly high number of them in the British Isles during the nineteenth century. Such people believed themselves to be oxen or cows, and behaved exactly like them, without fully forgetting their true identity.

It was to such a state that the Lord reduced the most powerful man in the world, both as a punishment for his pride, and as a means of teaching him a spiritual lesson which would bring about his conversion. His courtiers drove out their demented sovereign and surveyed him with wonderment as he ate grass and rolled in the dew, with uncut hair and nails. Who could have envisaged that such a thing could happen to the King of *Babylon*? The man to whom nothing appeared impossible had been reduced to utter helplessness. He who had always been regarded with servile fear was now the object of continual pity.

But there was a kind purpose in the divine judgement, and we have already surveyed the spiritual results of it, as they are recorded in verses 34 and 35. When God restored Nebuchadnezzar's reason, He also restored his kingdom to its previous glory. The counsellors who had been running the empire during his absence now came to him for advice and direction, just as they did before. The restored king was a man whose confession of faith is found in verse 37, and who ruled briefly as a godly king before dying shortly afterwards in fellowship with God.

God did it! He who was one thing before chapter 4 was quite another thing afterwards. The change was a divine change. God did it!

Our second point is to notice that God did it, not by boosting the man up, but by knocking him down. *That* is how God converts people!

One day the king is in his splendid Babylon, filled with pride and inflated by his own sense of achievement. In his majesty he looks round at the gardens, the temples and the magnificent buildings. He does not need anybody. He is a self-made man. Anything that he wants he can have. Anything that he commands is done at once.

Then, within an hour, he is clawing in the earth, like the oxen of the fields!

The weeks and the months go by. Seven 'times' go by — however long that may be. And little by little, even while he is searching in the ground and eating grass, he is beginning to realize something. Apparently completely demented, and behaving and sounding just like the animal that he considers himself to be, he has still sufficient inner consciousness to recognize truths that he should have grasped years before.

Things which he has heard, and to which he has assented, are coming back into his mind. Not in a moment, but nonetheless surely, he is coming to the realization that God is the only God, and that He is the King of heaven. Now he is sure that it is true. At last he comes to *fiducia,* and commits himself to the truth of which he has been persuaded. Never again will he live as if he, or any other man, is the centre of the universe. Never again will he fall into the trap of thinking that the world revolves around him.

From this moment onwards he will live as a subject to the true King. He will go to His throne like a suppliant. He will embrace that God as a little child would his father. When a person becomes a little child, he can see the kingdom of heaven (Matthew 18:3).

At last this great king is in the place where every man and woman should be. He is prostrate in the dust before God. His heart is changed, his reason is restored, and he comes back to his full manhood and former glory. He goes into eternity in fellowship with the King of heaven.

That is how his conversion took place. God did it! And *God did it*, not by boosting him up, but by knocking him down.

Two lessons to learn

The historical narrative which we have just read has two important lessons to teach us.

The first is that *we should never despair of the conversion of anybody.* Who would have thought that the powerful king, taking God's people captive and pressurizing God's remnant to join him in idolatry, would one day himself be in fellowship with that God? It was to a total pagan that the exiles bowed in 605 B.C. Surely it was impossible that he should ever become one of the people of God himself! But with God nothing shall be called impossible.

And when he was furious, angry and irrational, and commanding the execution of his wise men, who would ever have guessed that the man doing *that* would ever become a believer? It seemed even less likely when he turned his back on the truth which he had heard and commanded all his people to worship a hideous statue. Could the man who commanded that

God's remnant should be burned in a furnace ever become part of that remnant? It seemed out of the question.

But as our chapter closes we see him as a little child at God's feet. As a subject and as a suppliant, he is worshipping, praising, extolling and honouring the King of heaven!

While Nebuchadnezzar's God remains God we should never despair of the conversion of anybody. Very often we are tempted to question whether there is any point in continuing with Christian work. People around us seem intolerably hard or unbelievably apathetic. Almost everything seems more important to them than the things of God. Our message to them is either blandly ignored or cynically opposed. They are men and women, it seems, who will never break. It seems impossible that any of them could ever be converted. We find it hard to imagine that anyone could be further from God than they are.

We will capitulate into total despair if we forget that God is omnipotent. If He can crack a nut like Nebuchadnezzar, who will prove to be too difficult for Him? He has done what we call 'impossible' before, and He can do it again. As His co-workers it is our duty to keep on working for the conversion of all around us, trusting that His almighty power cannot finally be resisted by anyone whom He is determined to save. What we cannot, *He* can do! We must never despair of the conversion of anyone.

There is a second lesson to learn from this chapter, and I address it to any readers who are still unconverted. The reason why you are not saved, despite all your interest in the Bible, is because *you are not yet low enough.* You still think too much of yourself to come like a child to God. You are still too proud to come as a subject before the divine throne. Your own sense of importance prevents you from coming like a beggar to the King.

I must write frankly to you. It is time for you to face the fact that God will not save both you and your respectability. He will not save you without loss of face on your part. Those who come to God through Christ must come in the same way as all others before them have come.

The tax-collector would not lift up so much as his eyes to heaven and cried from his heart, 'God be merciful to me a sinner' (Luke 18:13). The great intellectual, Saul of Tarsus,

Daniel 4

came while he was still dithering and blind on the Damascus Road, with the prayer: 'Lord, what wilt though have me to do?' (Acts 9:6). The tough Philippian gaoler fell on his knees and implored, 'What must I do to be saved?' (Acts 16:30.)

The only way of approach to the Most High God is from the lowest place of all. The conversion of Nebuchadnezzar shows us that. And the Lord Jesus Christ saves people from that position, because He came not to call the righteous, but sinners to repentance (Mark 2:17).

The most merciful thing that God can do to a sinner is to knock him down. In that position a man or woman is always safe. The only way he can turn his eyes is upwards. The only place to which he can appeal is heaven.

A final warning

Those who are reluctant to fall at God's feet should heed a final warning. God has power to take away a person's reason. Who knows how God will react to your repeated rejections of His invitations and warnings? Perhaps He will break you beyond remedy (Proverbs 29:1). If He should take away your reason, and choose not to restore it, how would you call upon Him for mercy then? He gives you your reason today, so why not act on what you know to be true? Tomorrow He may say, 'Enough is enough,' and leave you without power even to know or to assent to His truth, let alone to rest upon it.

We must not fear to be broken by God. He only remakes what He has broken. He does not despise a broken and contrite heart (Psalm 51:17). Nor must we fear to be ruled by Him. All His works are truth, and His ways justice (37).

Shall we not, as we close this chapter, recall His greatness and admit our own nothingness? He has no welcome for those who believe themselves to be something. It is those with empty hands, and with nothing to plead, that He never turns away. His ear is deaf to prayers from human heights, but cries of despair from the depths ring loudly in His ears and always gain His attention. He does not expect us to live a perfect life before we please Him, for Christ our Saviour has lived it on our behalf. There is no penalty for Him to punish us with, because the Son whom He sent has carried it all. All cries of pride are a contradiction of these great truths. Only cries from the dust are consistent with them, and this is why Nebuchadnezzar had to be brought so low before he could enter into fellowship with Him.

Will you not now take out Nebuchadnezzar's name from the final verse, and make it your personal confession of faith? 'Now I ... praise and extol and honour the King of heaven, all whose works are truth, and his ways judgement: and those that walk in pride he is able to abase.'

6.
HOW TO BE LOST

Please read Daniel chapter 5

Nebuchadnezzar was an incredibly wicked man, but everything worked out all right for him in the end. This is because God humbled him, and the once proud king became His subject.

But it does not always work out all right for wicked people. This is the lesson of Daniel chapter 5.

The road which unconverted people walk has an invisible line across it — a line seen by God alone, and not by us. God is patient and long suffering with those who neglect and despise Him. He gives them many opportunities to turn to Him. He invites them to come to Him, and pleads and beseeches and persuades. His consistent desire is that the unconverted should turn around and seek Him, rather than continue to walk away from Him.

Those who persist in walking the road that they have chosen one day cross the invisible line. They cross the thin boundary between God's patience and His wrath. At last He says, 'Enough is enough,' and gives them up. There is no special road which leads to hell. You just have to stay on your present road long enough.

Men and women are not lost because they are great sinners. The Lord Christ is well able to save the greatest of sinners. Nor do people go to eternal torment because of the number or frequency of their sins. There are great sinners in hell, and also what people call 'little' sinners. Men and women perish because during their lifetime their hearts are pockets of resistance to God, and they walk their own way until God's patience runs out. Stifling their conscience again and again, they arrive at the point where God has nothing more to say to them. They never humbly seek His mercy. They never approach the appointed Saviour, but remain stubborn, arrogant and self-willed. Men and women are lost through lack of abasement and prostration.

This chapter powerfully brings home this lesson to our hearts. It does so by introducing us to five characters, the first of whom is in verses 1 to 4.

Belshazzar

'Belshazzar' means 'Bel, protect the king' and is, of course, a pagan name. In the past many cynics have asserted that this story is fictional and that Belshazzar never existed, but the cuneiform documents of the Middle East have now silenced them. There is no longer any question regarding Belshazzar's historicity. As is always the case, the Bible was right and the critics were wrong.

Our chapter calls Belshazzar 'the king', but he was not the *only* king. At that time Nabonidus was the King of Babylon and Belshazzar was his co-regent. He had all the rights, prerogatives and majesty of the king, except in one point. In the official inscriptions of the realm Nabonidus was always called 'the king', and Belshazzar was given a lesser title. If you like, he was a sort of 'junior' king! As far as the day-to-day practicalities of rule were concerned, he was a co-king, and he and Nabonidus had a harmonious relationship together. If there were any disputes between them Nabonidus would have had the final word, but we do not know of any such occurrence. They ruled as coequals over the vast empire of Babylon.

Like Nabonidus, Belshazzar was the son of Nebuchadnezzar — though there is an outside possibility that he was the son (or adopted son) of Nabonidus, and that the word 'father' in this chapter is used in the sense of 'ancestor' or 'grandfather' (as the Authorized Version margin has it at verse 2).

This means that he had lived as a boy and as a youth through the stirring events of the first four chapters of Daniel. When Nebuchadnezzar discovered that four young men were exceptional, and that they were also worshippers of Jehovah, Belshazzar witnessed it. He would have heard Daniel's God-given interpretation of his father's horrific dream. He would have joined in the wonderment brought about by Shadrach, Meshach and Abed-nego's walk with the Son of God in the flames of the furnace. He would have seen his father become like an animal, and would have known how he had spent his last days on earth with a personal faith in the living God whom he had failed to worship for so long.

Belshazzar had virtually grown up alongside Daniel and his three companions. They were only fourteen when they were exiled, and the age gap between them could not have been very wide. Perhaps he had heard Daniel pray or preach. He had certainly seen him stand out for God.

We are faced in this chapter with a man who had been exposed to a living testimony to the true God from his early years. We must never think that Nebuchadnezzar had been the only person in Babylon who had been exposed to God's truth; Belshazzar had had the same experience. Like his father, he had had the opportunity to get right with God. The Saviour had knocked at his heart through the events he had witnessed. He was a man who had seen God having personal dealings with someone close to him. He knew what conversion was, for he had seen his own father become a subject to Jehovah. The true God had been both worshipped and adored in the palace which he now occupied as king.

This is the man who now throws a feast for a thousand of his dignitaries!

It has come to the point where God's patience with Belshazzar is running out. Far from submitting to God, he continues to resist him. He remains unbroken, and the day of reckoning is about to come. Unknown to him, one more step along the path of ungodliness will bring him over the invisible line. He will take but one more pace away from God, and God will present him with His account. One more act of contempt for God will cause that God to declare, 'Enough!' The day of his opportunity to repent is fast coming to an end. We *cannot* go as far as we like in sinning, and the story of Belzhazzar will prove this to us. One more sin, and it will be all up with him!

The occasion for his final sin is an enormous drinking party. Such events were quite common in ancient Babylon. A great dignitary would invite other V.I.P.s to come together with no other purpose than that of getting drunk. It was a time for gaudy and lewd songs and unrestrained behaviour. The evening ended with the guests being helped home, to boast next morning that they had had 'a good time'.

The effects of drunkenness are well known, and the Word of God repeatedly speaks out against it. As the drink begins to take effect on Belshazzar he throws all decency and propriety to the wind. He tells the whole revelling crowd that they are to join him in desecrating the vessels which his father had brought from Jehovah's temple when he had captured Jerusalem. They are going to booze themselves out of the vessels which had been consecrated to the worship of the only God. As they do so, drunken songs are sung in praise of Babylonian idols. The scene is one of drunken contempt for the God of heaven — the God of whom Belshazzar has heard from childhood, and to whose witness he has been exposed. The king puts the golden vessels in the hands of his guests and leads the revelry as they scorn the holy and applaud the contemptible. 'They drank wine, and praised the gods of gold, and of silver, of brass, of iron, of wood, and of stone' (4).

The fingers of a man's hand

The second character in this narrative is the finger of a man's hand. We read of this in verses 5 to 9.

How many times have we seen supposed pictures of this scene! In almost every case our books portray the writing as being done by a whole hand. But it was not. It was the 'fingers of a man's hand ... the part of the hand that wrote' (5). In our imagination we can both see and hear the laughter and the merriment. The note is now one of hilarity and wild debauchery as drunken voices chant base songs in praise of pagan deities. Sin is rampant and unashamed and parades itself as enjoyable. The atmosphere is one of unrestrained godlessness, and there is nothing to spoil its filthy progress.

Then there is a stunned and petrified silence!

That is how quickly God can change a situation. In the twinkling of an eye it is all up with the arrogant king. God has been noting all his thoughts, words and deeds. He has now caught up with him and is presenting His account!

Following Babylonian custom the banqueting hall would have had a small platform or stage at one end. This would have been very well lit with chandeliers and candelabra, for upon this stage was situated the royal table of the host. We know from archaeology that behind this royal dais would have been a white plaster wall. Every eye is now turned towards it, for, in the midst of their haughty and unashamed orgy a dark shape has moved across it. Nothing can be seen but the fingers of a man's hand. There is no man, no arm, and hardly a hand — just a few fingers. Four words stare everyone in the face. These, says the Aramaic of this chapter, were not written but *inscribed*! The royal wall resembles a gravestone, and the whole company has seen the epitaph being engraved upon it: MENE, MENE, TEKEL, UPHARSIN.

Wine-reddened faces become ashen, and none more so than the king's. Where now is the laughing, contemptuous and godless King of Babylon? With the colour drained from his cheeks and his conscience terrified, the mighty king wets himself with fear as his knees knock togther. In his terror he stammers out fantastic promises to anybody who can interpret the supernaturally written inscription. But nobody can. Not only are the characters unusual, but spiritual enlightenment will be necessary to understand the message left behind by the unearthly fingers. Such a quality is not to be found in a boozing-house.

So the party is ended. Four words from God have reduced it to panic, to fear, to terror and to confusion. When the wicked do the most wicked things that they can think of, 'He that sitteth in the heavens shall laugh: the Lord shall have them in derision' (Psalm 2:4). We should certainly fear God, but never the wicked.

The queen

The third character to appear in the narrative is the queen (10–12). This is not any of Belshazzar's wives, because they are already at the feast, as verses 2 and 3 have told us. Who then is this queen? This is the wife of Nabonidus. She can enter the royal banqueting-hall in her own right, and without the protocol required of others. Her husband is the first, and Belshazzar is the second, which explains why he promised the *third* place in the kingdom to whoever could interpret the writing on the wall.

Whatever Belshazzar has forgotten, the queen has not. In

verses 10 to 12 she speaks like the pagan she undoubtedly was. But she recognizes that Daniel has supernatural wisdom. He has only to be called and the interpretation of the words will be known. He has the gift of understanding riddles and of interpreting hard sentences.

If God had wished He could have given the interpretation to Belshazzar some other way. He could, for example, have sent the unearthly fingers a second time, to write the meaning of the original message underneath. But this is not God's way. He does not bypass human agency. His message is to be expounded by His servant. Human lips will bring home the message. The remnant will be involved, not because God *needs* to include them, but because His constant method is that faithful men and women should be co-workers together with Him. He will not proceed without them. *This* is how He keeps His truth alive in the world. The entrance of Daniel brings us to the fourth character in this chapter, of which he occupies the greater part. What is said of him is recorded in verses 13 to 29.

Daniel

The questions that Belshazzar asks Daniel in verse 13 confirm that he already knows a good deal about him. This serves to underline that his ignorance of the ways of God is a willing ignorance. He has been exposed to holy things from boyhood and when he becomes king he chooses not to have Daniel at court. He does not want a prophet of Jehovah at the palace. The last person he wants as his counsellor and confidante is God's chosen messenger. How different things might have been if he had had Daniel at court from the beginning of his reign!

Be that as it may, Daniel is now before him. In verses 14 to 16 we see him explaining the situation to the prophet, and promising to reward him if he will interpret what is written on the wall. We do not need much imagination to visualize the scene while Daniel considered his reply. A thousand terror-stricken lords are hushed. The tongues which so recently mocked the living God are stilled. A crowd of pale and perplexed courtiers waits with overwhelming expectancy to hear the man of God speak.

Daniel's opening comments are to tell the king that he rejects his gifts (17). Unlike the professional astrologers around him, he does not give interpretations in the hope of personal gain. He is not a seeker of rewards or favours. He is not in it for the money. Such comments as these must have made their own impression upon the people — as they still do, when God's servants show no interest in the world's honours. It is clear that, come what may, Daniel is going to tell the truth. He cannot be bribed to say what the assembly wants to hear. Nor can he be bought off, so that what is offensive is avoided. The interpretation will be a true one.

Daniel continues by talking about Belshazzar's father. 'O thou king, the most high God gave Nebuchadnezzar thy father a kingdom, and majesty, and glory, and honour ...' (18).

Belshazzar is only a co-regent, a co-king. The empire is not what it used to be. In its history there had never been anyone greater than Nebuchadnezzar, but he owed all that he had to the Most High God. Greater than Nebuchadnezzar is God! This Nebuchadnezzar was responsible to Him for the exercise of his power — and look what God did to him! Daniel reminds Belshazzar of the way in which God humbled his father, 'Till he knew that the most high God ruled in the kingdom of men, and that he appointeth over it whomsoever he will' (21).

It is as if Daniel was saying, 'You, Belshazzar, have behaved as if you were the greatest person who has ever lived. But greater than you was your father, and greater than him is *God*! It was God who gave him everything that he ever had. There is a most high God, and although you may be the man on earth to whom all others are answerable, you yourself are answerable to this God. Everything that you have has been given to you by Him, and He can take it away just as easily. This applies even to your reason.

'You knew all this, Belshazzar. You knew how God humbled your father until he became His suppliant, but you did not follow his example. You behaved as an independent and unanswerable man. Indeed, you have gone further. You have thrown down the gauntlet to the God of heaven. Look whom you have praised: "the gods of silver, and gold, of brass, iron, wood, and stone, which see not, nor hear, nor know"'.

'And look, Belshazzar, whom you have despised — "the God in whose hand thy breath is, and whose are all thy ways, hast thou not glorified" (23). *That* is why the part of a man's hand has come and inscribed that writing on the wall. It is a message from God!'

Belshazzar was condemned for his pride. Pride, in the Bible, is lack of prostration. A person who is not in the dust before God is a proud person. He may not appear to be proud to his colleagues. She may pass as quite humble among her neighbours. The family may not notice. But a heart that is doing anything less than worshipping and adoring before God is a proud heart. Such pride is the characteristic of all men and women who are walking the path to hell. Belshazzar was a great sinner, but that is not the point at issue. His fault was that he would have nothing to do with the true and living God. He would not approach Him as a child, or have Him to rule over his life. He continued like that until he came to the point where he was willing to mock God. At that point he stepped over the line. We say it again — you do not have to choose a special road to go to hell; you just have to stay on your present road long enough.

The writing on the wall is preserved for us in verse 25. It consisted of three different words, one of which was written twice. MENE, MENE, means 'numbered, numbered'. That was followed by TEKEL, which means 'weighed'. After that came the word UPHARSIN.

PHARSIN is the plural of the word PERES. UPHARSIN is the word PERES in the plural, with the word 'and' in front of it. That is why to those of us who do not know Aramaic the interpretation appears to be different from the words which were written. When Daniel went through the words one by one, he went through them in their singular form. He did not go through them in the form in which they were inscribed on the plaster.

What was written on the wall, then, was 'Numbered, numbered, weighed and divided.' That was all that God had to say to unhumbled Belshazzar, but the full import of what it meant was now to be explained by godly Daniel.

'MENE means "numbered", because your days *are* numbered, King Belshazzar! God has decided to call a halt, and to bring your wicked kingdom to an end. Your period of rule is over. All these years God has been weighing it up, and now His time to finish it has arrived. He has said "Enough!", and your reign is ended — ended by God (26)!

'TEKEL means "weighed". Belshazzar, every action of your life has been weighed by God. He took note when, in boyhood, you rejected every opportunity to come to Him. He has recorded every invitation to become His subject which you have spurned. The fingers which God has sent have written your epitaph on the wall. No doubt as they did so your past life flashed before your mind. Your secret sins and open sins, your misspent hours, your cruelty, pride, wild disorders and drunkenness, your neglect of holy things and your spiritual resistance — God has weighed it all up. Each one has gone into His balance. He has considered your life from beginning to end, and it does not come up to the mark. It does not satisfy His standards' (27).

When people sneer at God, He does not ignore it. Because He does not act at once, wicked minds conclude that He will not act at all. He weighs up all their mockery and defiance in His balances. Nothing is forgotten. A record is kept of every invitation to come to Christ which is brushed aside. There is a note of every failure to take seriously His command to repent. All who lightly esteem the evangelical faith, who mock holy things, and especially those who reject the tenderness of their Maker, have their actions recorded in heaven. God notes it all.

'It is not for me,' say some. 'The cost is too great,' cry others. 'I don't want to be different. Everyone will think that I am a crank. They are a crowd of fanatics; I do not want to be an extremist. Why should I?' — these and all other comments are both heard and remembered by the ever-present God. At last God will take no more, and the writing appears on the wall. The day of trifling is over. It is now the day of damnation.

'PERES means "divided". Your kingdom is to be divided and destroyed. It will be brought about by the combined might of the Medes and the Persians. The kingdom is to be taken from you, Belshazzar, and is to be given to another' (28).

And it was not just that kingdom, was it? It was the kingdom of God that he ultimately lost. Our Lord Jesus Christ made a similar accusation to the Jews. He told them that they had turned away the prophets by stoning and killing them. At last they turned away God's son. God's response was to take away the vineyard from them and to give it to others (Matthew 21:33–43).

Paul repeated the same note. When the Jews rejected his gospel message, he warned them that God would take away their privileges, and would give them to the Gentiles (Acts 13:44–50). Something similar happens whenever the gospel is repeatedly and stubbornly rejected. God eventually says to the people concerned, 'Seeing you so obviously reject the only message which can save you, I am going to judge you by taking it away from you. Now if you seek repentence, even if you seek it with weeping, you will not be able to find it' (Hebrews 12:17).

An invisible line has been crossed into the land of no return. It is all up with the person concerned. There is no more opportunity to find mercy. All that now awaits him is 'a certain fearful looking for of judgement and fiery indignation' (Hebrews 10:27).

> There is a time, we know not when,
> A place we know not where,
> That marks the destiny of man
> In glory or despair.
>
> There is a line, by us unseen,
> That crosses every path,
> The hidden boundary between
> God's patience and His wrath.
>
> Oh, what is that mysterious bourn
> By which man's path is crossed,
> Beyond which God Himself hath sworn,
> The soul that goes is lost?
>
> How long might I go on in sin,
> How long will God forbear;
> Where does hope end and where begin
> The confines of despair?
>
> The answer from the skies is sent —
> 'Ye who from God depart,
> While it is called today, repent
> And harden not your heart.'

Darius

Despite Daniel's contempt for earthly rewards, they are given to him, because Belshazzar knows that he has heard the truth (29). But the whole thing is so short-lived, and this solemn chapter closes in verses 30 and 31 by introducing us to a fifth character — Darius.

The very night that Daniel spoke, Nabonidus' armies went out against the Medes and the Persians who were threatening Babylon's borders. But Cyrus the Persian moved in quickly. He diverted the River Euphrates and crossed it. By morning the Median and Persian armies had swept into Babylon and conquered it. Belshazzar was a corpse in the palace and hearing the condemnation of the Maker whom he had so boldly despised and mocked the night before. Daniel's prophecy was fulfilled, and God had demonstrated once more that He is the true Ruler of this world's history. The golden head gave way to the silver chest and arms, and sixty-two-year old Darius ascended the throne.

Who knows when God will say to a person, 'One more sin will be your last. Then the writing will be on the wall for you. I will snatch you into eternity while every voice in heaven joins me in saying, "Thou fool, this night thy soul shall be required of thee"'? (Luke 12:20.)

'Seek ye the Lord while he may be found, call ye upon him while he is near; let the wicked forsake his way, and the unrighteous man his thoughts: and let him return unto the Lord, and he will have mercy upon him; and to our God, for he will abundantly pardon' (Isaiah 55:6-7).

7.
IN THE LIONS' DEN

Please read Daniel chapter 6

We come now to the last of the historical chapters of the book of Daniel, for the ones which follow are composed of prophetical visions. It is one of the best known chapters in the whole of the Bible, and does not really need any introduction. It records an incident which took place when Daniel was an old man. In the opening chapter he was a youth of only fourteen, and we are able to see in this one how he remained true to God even in advanced years.

A plot to destroy Daniel

The chapter divides naturally into three sections, the first of which is contained in verses 1 to 9. It records a plot to destroy Daniel.

The narrative opens with a change of dynasty. The Babylonian Empire is now a thing of the past. It has been conquered by the combined might of the Medes and Persians, and the second great empire of Nebuchadnezzar's dream is now a fact of life. The first ruler of the new dynasty is an otherwise unknown Mede by the name of Darius, who ascends the throne at the late age of sixty-two. We know that he did not reign for very long, for when we put together the historical jigsaw we discover that Cyrus the Persian was reigning very shortly afterwards.

To Darius falls the difficult task of taking over the Babylonian Empire, and giving it a new direction and identity under the rule of the Medes and Persians. The administrative difficulties before him must have been immense, and the opening verses of the chapter reveal how he tackled them. He put the empire's affairs into the hands of one hundred and

Daniel 6

twenty satraps. Presumably each one took responsibility for a particular area. These were answerable to three presidents, 'that the king might suffer no loss' (2). The presidents, in turn, were responsible to the king himself. In this way Darius maintained his absolute power, and yet government did not remain at a distance from the people.

One of the three presidents was Daniel, and we read in verse 3 that he was so outstanding that the king thought of setting him over the whole realm. A shift in the hierarchy was contemplated, so that one of the presidents would be senior to the others, and would become the king's deputy.

How is that Daniel came immediately to a position of such eminence in the new regime? How could someone who was so prominent in the defeated dynasty come at once to such a high position in the government of those who conquered it? This question has often been regarded as impossibly difficult, but in the fact the answer is simple.

The empire which fell was like every other great empire which has fallen. It was degenerate. It was filled with a love of luxury and a lack of desire for hard work. There was a widespread abandonment of principles and an unrestrained increase in immorality and dishonesty. The moral climate was rotten. The officials of Babylon had generally become men who had little interest in anything except lining their own pockets, and feathering their own nests. The 'get-rich-quick' mentality ruled them so completely that they threw all their scruples to the wind and gave themselves to pursuing personal gain and advancement.

A change of government does not, of itself, bring about a change in the moral climate. Darius had no guarantee that the satraps whom he had appointed would be any different from the Babylonian officials that they had replaced. Perhaps they would stoop to the same tactics and be more interested in their own personal advantage than in the correct administration of the empire. It was therefore imperative that they should not easily be able to get their hands on public funds. To prevent this, Darius needed a man of unimpeachable honesty whom he could put in charge of the exchequer. If he could not find such a man it was likely that his whole administration would fall to pieces.

He recognized that he had the man he needed in Daniel. The

spirituality of the man guaranteed that he could be neither bribed nor bought (3). It is said today that every man has his price; but it was not that way with Daniel. The fear of God ruled in his heart, and he could be relied upon to be unquestionably loyal to the king. His honesty was beyond question. There was a moral excellence in the man, a spirit of unblemished integrity. Twisted officials would have to face the fact that there was an insuperable barrier between them and the abuse of public money. It was Daniel.

Perhaps some readers of this book mix in the business world. They will know that powerful men who want easy riches can be utterly ruthless in their pursuit of them. They will stop at nothing. They do not turn a hair if the realization of their ambitions means the destruction of smaller but honest businessmen. There is no depth to which they will not stoop for the prize of fat profits. There is no end to their inhumanity and callousness when it serves their own self-interest.

In the same way the one hundred and twenty satraps and the two other presidents resolved to get rid of Daniel (4). They knew that they would never be able to fault him as far as the discharge of his public duties was concerned. There was no chance. Daniel was everything that he should be. His testimony at work was beyond reproach — and he presents an example for all the Lord's people to follow. Therefore they had to hatch a plot of a very different sort. It would settle him once and for all, and get him out of the way. Very soon Daniel would be off the scene.

Their reasoning went something like this: 'Daniel is faithful to Darius because, first of all, he is faithful to his God. It is his spirituality which guarantees his integrity. One is the cause of the other ... If we can put him in a position where he has to choose between his God and the king, he will undoubtedly choose his God. In this way he will fall foul of the king, and will be out.'

With this sort of logic in their minds, they began to harness all their energies into arranging such a dilemma for Daniel.

Whenever a person stands for honesty and justice, it makes an impression. Such a person inevitably gets in the way of others, who come to hate him for it. Evil people still try to put godly people in the position where they must either be true to their God, and lose everything; or keep everything, and lose their distinctive testimony.

The tools which the plotters used were flattery and lies. These were exactly the tools which the devil used in the garden of Eden, and which he still uses today. He told Eve that by disobeying God she and her husband would be as gods. Flattery! He assured her that when she ate the forbidden fruit, she would not die. Lies! His tactics have remained unchanged because they usually prove to be successful.

The proposals which were made to the king must have flattered him greatly. It was suggested that for a period of thirty days he should be regarded as the earthly representative of whatever gods exist. It was further suggested that no prayer should be made to any gods at all, except through his mediation. No religion was to be banned or outlawed. Prayer to the various gods could go on as before, except that all such prayers and requests would have to be presented through Darius, and 'whosoever shall ask a petition of any God or man for thirty days, save of thee, O king, he shall be cast into the den of lions' (7).

No doubt the satraps and presidents gave Darius many good reasons why such a course of action should be adopted — it would be a uniting factor in the new empire; it would create respect for the new monarchy; it would establish the king's authority in all the affairs of his subjects, etc... All sorts of other reasons come to mind which could be suggested to a vain king as sufficient reason for such a decree to be made.

If the king had been a wise man, he would have smelled a rat immediately. But flattery has a marvellous effect. It boosts a person's pride and blinds him to the true issues. Darius was hearing his highest officials suggest that he should, in effect, be considered as a god. The suggestion was but one step removed from the deification of kings which characterized many ancient empires. The flattery caused him to overlook a detail of immense importance. No wonder that the Scriptures, and the book of Proverbs in particular, speak out so forthrightly against the flattering tongue!

What detail did the king overlook? He should have seen that the words of verse 7 were a patent lie. The claim was that '*All* the presidents of the kingdom ... have consulted together to establish a royal statute.' If that was so, why was Daniel, the most excellent of his presidents, not present when the suggestion was made? If all the senior officials were agreed on the proposals, why were they not being presented by the most senior official of all? Such thoughts should have passed through Darius' mind, but apparently did not do so. Shortly afterwards he signed the decree and, according to Medo-Persian custom, it became permanent law. Once signed, such royal laws could never be changed. Any attempt by Darius to do so would have caused massive upheaval in his empire, and he was not prepared for such a contingency at so early a stage in his reign.

We have seen how Nebuchadnezzar's command that everyone should bow to his image hurt nobody except the godly remnant. We have a parallel situation here. The whole Medo-Persian empire was composed of polytheistic idolaters. There was nothing about this new decree to trouble any of them. Their religions could go on, more or less unaffected. But not so Daniel. God's law forbade him to bow the knees to a man, or to recognize any other mediator than a divinely appointed one. There was no way by which he could both please his God and obey the king's edict.

The dilemma was acute. If Daniel prayed to Jehovah, in the way that he had always done, he was certain to incur the wrath of the king's edict. If he did not continue his lifelong practice of devotion to God, he was certain to lose his spirituality, and therefore also his integrity. He had to choose either to be a godly man who displeased the king and died, or an ungodly man who lived. Whichever way it was, it looked as if the wicked were going to triumph. In future there would either be no Daniel at all, or a Daniel who had sacrificed his principles and forsaken his previous character. It seemed that the plotters could not lose.

Daniel in the lions' den

The second section of our chapter is from verses 10 to 17, and even at this stage we will call it 'Daniel in the lions' den'.

When Daniel knew that the irrevocable edict had been signed, what did he do?

He did not do what most of *us* would have done. We would have panicked, or dramatically reacted in some other way. If a similar word of decree were passed today, most of us would run round to each other's houses, or would dash to the nearest airport in the hope of emigrating. Our hearts would be filled with the very worst sort of excitement.

What did Daniel do? He just carried on as normal, 'as he did aforetime' (10). He was unshaken, unmoved and unchanged.

The circumstances had certainly changed, but they did not change the man of God. It had been his habit to pray to God three times every day. He did it by the open windows of his residence which faced Jerusalem. He had been in exile a long time, but had not forgotten the city and country from which he had been stolen. Nor had he forgotten God's promise to restore Israel and to rebuild Jerusalem.

How is it that Daniel could be so public in his prayers? Does not our Lord tell us to go to our rooms, to bolt the door and to pray secretly to our heavenly Father? (Matthew 6:6.)

We need to remember that Daniel was an important public servant in an oriental empire. Servants would be scurrying throughout his home, and it is unlikely that he would have had very much privacy. There was no possibility of his keeping *his* devotions a secret. And now there were spies about, deliberately intent on discovering whether he maintained those private devotions during the period of the decree. His devotions had never been ostentatious, but nor had they ever been a secret. Carrying on as normal meant that they could not become a secret now.

Three times a day the man of God falls on his face before God, just as he has always done. The threat of death does not mean that he must stop doing what is right. Right is still right. Circumstances may alter, but God's absolutes do not. As we have stressed earlier, our duty in life is to do what is right, even though the heavens may fall. Consequences are God's responsibility.

But how is it that an old man can stand so firm, and display such courage and faith?

Such qualities do not come suddenly into a person's life. It was because he had developed a lifelong habit of saying 'No!' to evil that he was able to do it again in such desperate times.

If we want the explanation for chapter 6, verse 10, we must first read again chapter 1, verse 8. In that verse a young boy of fourteen 'purposed in his heart that he would not defile himself'. In his youth Daniel had refused to commit a comparatively small evil. Whatever had been the evils that he had encountered during the intervening years, his response had been a consistent refusal. He had developed an unflinching discipline of saying 'No!' to what is wrong.

Each time we say 'No!' to sin, we are that much more able to do so again next time. But each time we give in our resistance is weakened.

I suggest to you that the real den of lions was Daniel's bedroom. He knew that if he disobeyed the king's command, he would be mauled and savaged by wild animals, and would lose his life. But he would not have lost his testimony. As we have noted once before, the devil would prefer that we kept our lives and lost our testimonies.

It is therefore certain that whenever Daniel sank to his knees to pray, he would have been diabolically tempted. We can easily imagine what would have run through his mind. 'Why don't you make things easy for yourself? Look at the position you have, and the privileges you enjoy. Look at the influence you can continue to exert if you hold on to your present status. Make sure of the future by not praying to God over the next thirty days. Why sacrifice your long-term future on the altar of a short-term enjoyment of prayer? Pray secretly in your heart, if you like, but why do it in the way that you have always done it? You are sure to be noticed and to lose everything. Is it such a matter of principle? Is it really worth it? At least you could go and pray where neither the spies nor the household servants are likely to see you. Why make an issue of being *seen* to pray? After all, in just thirty days the danger will be over, and you can carry on just as you did before.'

This temptation would have come to Daniel at morning, and at midday and again in the evening. His mind would have heard a thousand plausible reasons why he should leave off what he was doing. Who can tell how wearying such daily and repeated temptation must have been?

There are many strong believers who cannot be knocked down by strong and sudden temptation, but whose resistance can be eroded away. It is a known tactic of the Evil One to seek to wear out the saints of the Most High (Daniel 7:25). He knows well enough that constant dripping wears away stone. Much of his temptation is therefore not violent, but subtle and

Daniel 6

gentle. He brings the same suggestions again and again and again, until it makes an impression. He sows the idea that a certain sin may not be harmful, and that it can actually be helpful. Evil as he is, he is well able to appear as an angel of light. More often than not a believer's resistance crumbles before such approaches and his testimony is ruined.

This well-tried tactic was entirely unsuccessful with Daniel. The pressure of this daily temptation was his real trial. It was his real den of lions. But on each occasion he said 'No!', fell to his knees, 'and prayed, and gave thanks before his God, as he did aforetime' (10).

The spies saw an unbroken consistency in Daniel. He was the same as before. Nothing had moved him; he was as firm as ever. We must surely agree that his adamant refusal to be intimidated by threats, or to give in to the devil's subtle suggestions, was a greater miracle than his later deliverance from the mouths of lions.

When it became plain that Daniel was not heeding the king's decree, the plotters set in motion the wheels that would lead to his execution. Their first step was to report him to the king (12). As they did so they made no mention whatever of his known integrity. Not a syllable was uttered in commendation of his honesty, or of how well he had fulfilled his responsibilities in his present high position. Instead the plotters remind the king that Daniel is nothing more than a captive exile, and insinuate that he is politically unfaithful and disloyal. Such bias and lack of balance is typical of the way in which wicked people act.

Daniel had promised Nebuchadnezzar that the kingdom following his would be inferior (2:39). The events that follow show just how true that prediction was. Nebuchadnezzar had been an absolute monarch, but we now see Darius caught up in the web of his own laws, and being manipulated by his courtiers and counsellors. The king of the empire has made a fool of himself!

He has put his pen to something that he has not seriously considered. He is now living to regret it, but cannot do anything about it. His dilemma is terrible. His own law condemns Daniel, and yet everything in his heart longs to save him. In his own stupidity he has made a decree which condemns the man of God, while his deepest personal desire is to save him. He searches all day for some legal loophole by which Daniel's life can be spared, but is rudely reminded by the plotters that he cannot go back on his edict. The wicked are calling the tune, and winning the day.

Many who have written books on Daniel ask us to pause at this point, to consider 'another Law and another Love' (Gaebelein). There was a *just* law which condemned us. Yet the One who gave that law yearned with a heart of love to save us. Divine wisdom solved the dilemma by sending the Lord Jesus Christ into the world. The demands of the divine law were kept by Him, on our behalf — both in terms of keeping it, and in bearing the punishment for breaking it. God resolved the dilemma in the life, death and resurrection of His Son.

But there was no solving of Darius's dilemma. He is nothing more than a weak and anaemic king who has made an ill-considered decree and is now bemoaning his own stupidity. He cries pitifully as he commits Daniel to the den of lions, expressing his deepest hope that God will step in to deliver him. His heart has no love for the law he has made. Yet he has to witness the ultimate irony. A seal is put on the entrance to the lions' den, to make it plain to all that Daniel has been placed there on the king's authority, and that any attempt to release him would be an act of treasonable defiance of the king's word.

The plotters undoubtedly rejoiced as they went home, but not so the king. Before him was a sleepless night. No food interested him, and he knew that there was no music which could take his mind off the folly of his actions. All his thoughts were of his loved and trusted Daniel, locked up in the lions' den.

Daniel was in great physical danger, but we need to remember that he was not in any spiritual danger. He had faced the devil squarely, and by doing so had escaped entirely out of his clutches. The Evil One had no hold of any sort on Daniel. He had no victory of any kind, nor did he, in any sense, have Daniel in his power. 'Resist the devil, and he will flee from you,' says the Word of God (James 4:7), and Daniel had proved the truth of these words before they were written. His integrity and spirituality remained unaffected and intact. His example needs to be noted by us all.

The *only* way to escape the devil is to face up to him. There is no other way to avoid falling into his clutches, and to remain free from his power: 'Whom resist stedfast in the faith' (1 Peter

Daniel 6

5:8-9). Daniel's forthright 'No!' to temptation has forced the devil to leave him alone. It is true that he is in the den of lions, but at least he does not have to endure satanic company there. As we shall see in a few moments, the company was *much* better!

Daniel's deliverance and the final outcome

The remainder of the chapter from verse 18 onwards tells us the great story of Daniel's deliverance and the final outcome.

After his sleepless night, Darius is back at the den of lions at the crack of dawn. There is a hole in the top of the den, so that spectators can see what is happening below. It is through this hole that he cries lamentably, his voice filled with anxiety: "Has the God who preserves life been able to preserve you, Daniel?" (20). He is not really expecting any reply, and expects to see the remains of God's servant who has horribly perished in the night.

'O king, live for ever', replies a steady voice which he never expected to hear again. The voice of the man who all thought to be dead is courteously wishing *him* life!

With what overwhelming joy did he hear out the reply! 'My God has seen that I am innocent both of offending Him and of wronging you. He has sent His angel into the den here and He has firmly shut the lions' mouths. I am completely untouched.'

Daniel had not known the company of the devil in the night, because he had fled from him. But he *had* known the company of the Lord Jesus Christ! The Angel of the Lord, who led Jacob through his long life, the Angel who accompanied Shadrach, Meshach and Abed-nego in the fiery furnace — the same Angel had blessed Daniel with His company during the night hours. He who was in later years to display His authority over the winds and waves had that night displayed His authority over the lions and had restrained all their natural instincts to savage and kill the victim who had been presented to them!

Darius cannot wait until the seal is taken off the side door through which the lions had come in. Ropes are put down at once and, it appears, Daniel is pulled out of the top. They lift him up and out and examine him meticulously. There is not a scratch on him! Nor is his hair standing on end!

Once more God has not delivered His servant *from* trouble, but *in* trouble, just as He did with those in the fiery furnace. It was the same with the apostle Paul. What a catalogue of suffering he gives us in 2 Corinthians 11:23-33! Yet, in the very context of suffering, he had become persuaded that there was nothing that could separate him from his Saviour (Romans 8:35-39). Ours will be the same experience. All who want to live godly Christian lives can be certain of persecution (2 Timothy 3:12). It is simply not true that God undertakes to deliver us from difficulty and from painful and terrifying experiences. But it *is* true that He will deliver us *in* the difficulty, even in martyrdom. There is no situation into which we shall ever enter without Christ. And there is no suffering, even martyrdom, from which we shall not emerge alive!

Wicked people have no such consolations with which to garrison their hearts. This truth is emphasized by verse 24. It is an awful verse. The plotters are now thrown to their doom and, in accordance with Persian practice, so are their wives and children. It is a horrific scene.

The Scriptures do not say that this was commanded by God. It was the command of an unconverted king, and the Word of God does not commend him. But it does record the fact. As soon as the evil plotters and their poor wives and children were thrown into the den, they were torn limb from limb by the viciousness of the lions. The awful scene should distress us. It should also serve to underline in our minds how miraculous was Daniel's deliverance from the same pit. *God* did it!

This was something that Darius was brought to recognize, as is clear from his decree which closes the chapter. Writing to all the peoples of his realm, he there confesses God to be the greatest God, although, like Nebuchadnezzar after the fiery furnace incident, he does not confess Him as the *only* God.

Spiritual blindness is an awful thing. A man can come to see that God is great, that His dominion is everlasting and that His kingdom is endless. He can be brought to fear and tremble before the God whom he knows to live. He can actually acknowledge that this God does as He pleases in both heaven and earth. And yet he can fail to understand that God is the only God, and can live and die without any personal allegiance to Him. This is the way it was with Darius.

And so Darius passed from the stage of history. The Mede

was replaced by Cyrus the Persian (28). Kings come and go, as do empires. The remnant remains. That is the main lesson of this chapter and it should never fail to hearten and encourage us.

But what if the salt loses its savour? Every day this tiny remnant is faced with the choice of either pleasing its God, or pleasing others. It is told that only by pleasing others can it hope to survive; but if it should do that, it knows that it will lose its testimony. The individuals concerned would no doubt live a little longer, but the godliness of the remnant, which *makes* it the remnant, would be gone. If a witness to God is to be maintained in the world it is essential that the remnant should give no thought to its physical survival, but only to its spiritual purity.

A concern for spiritual purity — a consistent refusal to do *any* evil — makes the lions' den a certainty for those who are true to the Lord. But they can be certain of fellowship with Christ there, and that His power will ensure the physical survival of as many as are necessary for His witness to continue. In any event, even in the event of martyrdom, all faithful people can be sure of emerging from their trials *alive*!

One day it will be the turn of the wicked to go into the den. This will not be the den of a plotter's malice, but the den of the righteous indignation of God. When the wicked go there, they will go alone. They will know nothing of the divine presence and nothing of His rescue. Their punishment will be for ever and for ever and for ever.

What a difference there is between an unbeliever and a believer! The unbeliever prefers to endure the pains of hell for ever than to endure persecution for Christ and His gospel in this present life. By contrast, the believer considers that communion with God is the most precious thing in the world. He would rather have that than life itself and affirms constantly, 'I reckon that the sufferings of this present time are not worthy to be compared with the glory which shall be revealed in us' (Romans 8:18).

8.
AN INTERMISSION

Before we proceed to the next six chapters of Daniel it is necessary for us to have a short intermission. We need to stand back and look at these six chapters as a whole. Only then will we be in a position to examine them one by one.

Apocalyptic

This is because the second half of Daniel is quite different from the first. The most obvious difference is a change in style. The first six chapters were narrative and history and therefore exceptionally easy to follow. The next six chapters are mostly *apocalyptic.*
  Whatever is that?
  This is a distinct type of Jewish literature, of which the chapters that follow are the earliest example. Great quantities of it were produced by the Jews between 200 B.C. and A.D. 100. Those books were not divinely inspired and are therefore not found in our Bibles. But there are apocalyptic passages in several of the prophets, and good examples are Isaiah 24-27, Joel, and Zechariah 9-14. New Testament examples are our Lord's Olivet discourse in Matthew 24 and, supremely, the book of Revelation.
  Most apocalyptic literature was written to encourage faithful people in times of persecution. The main themes are always the same — the growth of evil, God's care for His people, and the assurance that evil will not finally prevail. The only thing of eternal duration is the kingdom of God.
  All apocalyptics claim to be revelations from God, given in an extraordinary manner, usually by visions and dreams. This is how the first apocalyptic writings came into being, and it

An intermission 87

does not surprise us that the claim is carried over into the non-inspired books. All of them, to a greater or lesser degree, are based on the exciting chapters that we are about to study.

The most noticeable feature of apocalyptic literature is its symbolism. In Daniel 7-12 the future course of history is going to be outlined to the prophet by means of numbers, beasts and horns. The language is mysterious. Indeed, at times it is almost bizarre. But when we are tempted to think that it is unnecessarily extravagant, it is worth remembering that it is modesty itself compared with the counterfeit apocalypses of later years. There the language is little short of wild, and the anonymous authors succeed in importing whole zoos into their supposed visions. The Word of God is free from such fanciful extremes.

Apocalyptic literature is always history written under the guise of prophecy. Of course, in the case of biblical apocalyptic writings this history was genuinely predictive. Future events were recorded before they occurred. Non-biblical apocalyptic writings are strikingly different. The events were already past when the authors wrote and they simply recorded what had already happened. They then appended the name of an author who had long since died and tried to pass off the whole thing as a genuine prophecy. Nobody was fooled for long. The only apocalypses not subsequently proved to be fakes are those which are found in the pages of the Bible — a further demonstration that God's Word has a heavenly origin, and is entirely distinct from merely human inventions.

We come, then, to chapters which predict trouble ahead for the godly. They will always live in a hostile and persecuting world. But they should not die of discouragement. History is in God's hands. All events are steadily bringing His purposes to pass. In His own time He will end the rule of evil and bring in His everlasting kingdom.

Purpose

With these things in mind, the overall purpose of chapters 7-12 should already be beginning to dawn on us. People who stand alone for God need encouragement. It is not enough for them to know how to stand alone; they also need to know *why* it is worthwhile. This is something which becomes clear when the believer knows a little about the future history of the world and has some understanding of God's unfolding plan for the ages.

After all, the chapters we are about to study had a wonderful effect on Daniel himself. For instance, in chapter 5 we saw him standing completely alone in the blasphemous court of Belshazzar and predicting both the imminent death of the king and the immediate take-over of the Babylonian Empire by the Medes and Persians. Who can possibly imagine what courage it required to say such things? From where did Daniel get the strength to do it? Why did he consider that he must speak the truth, even if it meant losing his own life?

We shall understand something of the answer when we have read chapters 7 and 8. Chapter 7 records a dream and chapter 8 a vision. The dream predicted the rise and fall of the same empires as those in Nebuchadnezzar's dream of chapter 2. Daniel came to see that human history is regulated by a heavenly court — a court which decrees that only the reign of the Lord Jesus Christ will last for ever. The vision which followed the dream concerned the more immediate future. It stressed that the forthcoming Medo-Persian Empire would give way to the Greek Empire, from which there would arise an awful persecutor of God's people, whom God would ruin at the peak of his influence.

All this Daniel saw before he ever set foot in Belshazzar's palace on that fateful night. Twice over he had been reminded that all events in human history do nothing but serve God's purposes. It was decreed *by God* that the Babylonian Empire should be followed by that of Medo-Persia. Why then should he be afraid to declare the fact to Belshazzar? Twice over he had been reminded that evil cannot possibly win the day. Why then should he be afraid to withstand it? The visions of chapters 7 and 8 showed him *why* standing alone for God is worthwhile.

The revelations given in chapter 9 did exactly the same thing. These were given by the angel Gabriel as Daniel was at prayer during the first year of Darius' reign. Is the prayer of chapter 9 one of those which he prayed during the difficulties recorded in chapter 6? In any event, it shows us something of the content of the prophet's prayers and sheds further light on why his windows were open towards Jerusalem.

An intermission

As a result of Gabriel's revelations Daniel knew for certain that the Jews would return to Palestine, rebuild Jerusalem and eventually witness the coming of the Messiah. There was a future for God's people. Should he, then, be ashamed of belonging to them? Should he not rather make it obvious that he was on God's side, even if it meant losing his life? Evil has no future, so what is the point of capitulating to it?

There was also another consideration. Daniel's experience in chapter 9 showed him that God answers prayer, sometimes even by angelic visitations. If a prayer can be heard from a bedroom, why not from a lions' den? And could not an angel come just as easily there, too? In the event, of course, that is precisely what happened.

But what about chapters 10-12? These constitute a single vision which Daniel received when he was at least eighty-six years old. We can see how chapters 7-9 helped him when he had to stand alone, but what practical effect did the final vision have? It came at a time when the aged prophet was nearing the end of his life.

Many elderly and mature believers are sometimes haunted by doubts. The devil does not cease to tempt us just because we have reached an advanced age! Is it possible that the saintly Daniel went through such an experience? Did he ever ask himself whether it had been worth living the whole of his life as the 'odd man out'? Had he wasted his time by standing alone? Would it not, perhaps, have been better to have compromised?

If such thoughts ever crossed his mind, the final vision recorded in chapters 10-12 would quickly have dispelled them. This time he saw not only some of the holy angels, but the Son of God Himself, and saw with fresh emphasis that human history is ruled by God even to its very end. The vision contained a detailed prediction of the history of the Greek Empire, and very especially of the wicked career of Antiochus Epiphanes. Daniel knew that after his death the people of God would have to face unspeakable persecution, not only from Antiochus, but also from the Antichrist during the last hours of this world's affairs. He also saw that it is God's principle to break evil when it is at its *height*. Evil will win many battles, but will never win the war. It will never ultimately triumph. God is God, and cannot be defeated. Only those who have been faithful to Him will have a glorious resurrection and an eternal rest.

This being so, how could Daniel ever have any regrets about walking so lonely a path for so long?

What these final visions did for Daniel himself, they have also done for countless readers ever since. Again and again, men and women have testified that they learned from the first six chapters *how* to stand alone for God, but it was from the second six chapters they learned *why* it was worthwhile. An early example of this is provided by the faithful Jews who were persecuted during the reign of Antiochus Epiphanes (175-164 B.C.). During the darkest years the book of Daniel was their principal comfort, and hundreds of secret copies were made and distributed widely. There can be no doubt that the encouragement that this book gave was the main reason why so many of them did not yield to the power of evil. How could they? They knew from these prophetic visions that Antiochus was doomed, as is all evil.

Scores of generations have come and gone since that time, but all over the world there are still believers who have to stand alone for God. Perhaps *you* have to do it, at home, at school or college, or at work. If so it is likely that a question will frequently have crossed your mind. You will often have asked, 'Where is it all going to end? Everybody around me seems to live as if there is no God, no Christ, no Bible, no death and no judgement. Where is it all going to end?'

Sometimes we come to the place where we say, 'Is there any point in going on? Here I am, trying to live true to God, but all that I ever seem to get is rough treatment. Round every corner there seems to be a fiery furnace or a lions' den. Whatever I do, and however well I live, my life seems to be one of constant trouble. Is there any point in going on as a persecuted minority?'

Thank God, it *is* worth going on! The next six chapters will convince us of it. They will show us why. That is their purpose.

Contents and interpretation

We should have gleaned from the preceding section that these six closing chapters do not present us with six mountains to cross, but only with three.

An intermission

Chapters 7 and 8 form the two sides of the first mountain. Chapter 7 is the vision of four great beasts which come out of the sea. The first three are easily recognizable as a lion, bear and leopard. But the fourth defies description and has ten horns. Very soon, however, it is forgotten, and the chapter focuses on an eleventh horn which follows the others and displaces some of them. This is not the only focus of the chapter. Also clearly in its view is a heavenly court which rules history, and which ensures that no one except the One 'like the Son of man' will reign eternally.

Whatever does all this mean? Fortunately, the book of Daniel is self-interpreting and never leaves us in the dark about the gist of what it is saying, even if many points of detail are not clear. In this case there is an obvious parallel between the four sections of the image in Nebuchadnezzar's dream (chapter 2) and the four beasts succeeding one another. Both span the time from the Babylonian Empire to the establishment of Christ's kingdom, and the empires in between. We did not find chapter 2 hard to understand, and chapter 7 is no more difficult — except for the question of the ten horns, and the eleventh, which are new features.

The other side of this first mountain is chapter 8. This is a vision concerning a ram with two horns (specifically said to be Medo-Persia), defeated by a he-goat from the west (specifically said to be Greece). The vision goes no further than the Greek Empire, and pauses to concentrate on a 'little horn' which emerges from it. This 'little horn' of chapter 8 is not to be identified with that of the previous chapter, for he does not emerge from the fourth empire, but from a division of the third. We shall see that the chapter is here speaking of Antiochus Epiphanes, and shall enquire why the same terminology is used both of him and the figure predicted by chapter 7.

Our second mountain is chapter 9. There we shall read that, while searching the Scriptures, Daniel came across Jeremiah's prophecy that the Babylonian exile would last only seventy years, and calculated that the time was nearly up. He therefore set himself to seek God's mercy on the Jews, with a view to their return to Palestine. Before he had finished praying, he received a visit from the angel Gabriel, assuring him that the Jews would indeed return. They would rebuild Jerusalem and would eventually witness the coming of the Messiah.

For these predicted events Gabriel gave a time-scale of 'seventy weeks'. Over the years there has been considerable disagreement as to precisely what Gabriel meant, and the last four verses of chapter 9 are rightly regarded as the most difficult verses in the whole book. This has frightened some people away from the chapter, and made them reluctant to study *any* of it. We shall not impoverish ourselves in this way, but we will be careful not to suggest that we, and we alone, have solved all the problems which the closing verses present.

This brings us to our third and final mountain, chapters 10-12. These contain a lengthy vision which Daniel received as an old man. Chapter 10 introduces the vision and tells us of the circumstances in which it was given. We learn that this final revelation came from the Lord Jesus Christ Himself! The elderly prophet had to be supernaturally strengthened to receive it.

To begin with, the vision overlaps with that of chapter 8. It explains that the Persian Empire will be followed by that of Greece. The prediction becomes increasingly detailed as it proceeds. It traces the rise and fall of Alexander the Great and the relationship of the two eastern sub-divisions which followed his death. Once more our eyes are brought to focus on the career of Antiochus Epiphanes, and on the atrocities which he was to commit against the people of God. But in looking at him we soon find ourselves looking at someone *like* him, an arch-persecutor of godly people who will occupy the centre of the world's stage at the end of history. At last we come to understand fully why both Antiochus and this coming figure can both be spoken of in the same breath. One is a prefigurement of the other and, as we saw in chapters 7 and 8, both can be described as 'little horns'.

But we do not close the book overawed by the power of evil. We are assured that its power is certain to be broken finally, and that those who have been faithful to God are certain of a blissful resurrection and of everlasting glory. The very last words are an exhortation to Daniel to continue in spiritual living, and we shall have understood the prophetical chapters well enough if they bring us to the same practical conclusion.

9.
THE VISION OF THE FOUR BEASTS

Please read Daniel chapter 7

We come, then, to the vision of the four beasts. We must not be discouraged if we cannot decipher every detail of what follows, for we shall find that the broad sweep of the chapter is as clear as crystal and that its main lesson is too obvious to be missed. Chapter 7 is a faith-building chapter. No Christian can fail to be strengthened by studying it, and most believers find it thoroughly exciting.

What Daniel saw

First of all, we look at what Daniel saw. This is in the first half of the chapter, and occupies verses 1 to 14.

Chapter 6 had taken place in the reign of Darius the Mede. However, the events of this chapter took place before then (1). The Babylonian Empire was still standing, and it was the first year of Belshazzar.

Lying on his couch at night, Daniel had a dream. Very often we forget our dreams as soon as we wake up, while on other occasions we remember them all day, and sometimes for months afterwards. When Daniel woke up, he wrote down this particular dream (1). He left out the secondary details, but recorded the main contents, 'the sum of the matters'.

The dream starts with four winds from the north, south, east and west all blowing at the same time upon the ocean and stirring it up. This ocean signifies mankind, because what emerges from it is something that emerges from mankind. This is clear from verse 17.

From the stormy ocean comes a succession of four beasts, each one quite different from the others. The first is described in verse 4: 'The first was like a lion, and had eagle's wings: I beheld till the wings thereof were plucked, and it was lifted up from the earth, and made stand upon the feet as a man, and a man's heart was given to it.'

That first beast corresponds to the head of gold of chapter 2, and is Babylon in the days of Nebuchadnezzar. The symbol of a lion with wings is well known in excavations in Babylon. As we know from chapter 4, a great change came over the empire of Babylon. It started off animal-like, but before it ended became decidely humanized. It was a much more compassionate kingdom towards its close.

The reason for the change was the conversion of Nebuchadnezzar. Nonetheless, as Babylon became humanized it also lost a great deal of its power. It could no longer fly over the whole earth like a bird of prey, consuming whomever it chose. A much more human heart was beating in it. The first beast of the vision is undoubtedly Babylon.

This is followed by a second beast from the ocean, as described in verse 5: 'And behold another beast, a second, like to a bear, and it raised up itself on one side, and it had three ribs in the mouth of it between the teeth of it: and they said thus unto it, Arise, devour much flesh.'

The picture is of a bear with both the legs of one side off the ground. It is an ungainly posture, but it means that the animal is ready to go forward. This is the empire of the Medes and Persians, and corresponds to the second part of the vision of chapter 2. When Daniel had this dream in the first year of King Belshazzar of Babylon, the Medo-Persian Empire was just about to march forward and to break upon the scene.

I simply do not know what the three ribs in the bear's mouth signify. We are in a symbolic section of the book, and we must always entertain the possibility that the numbers are symbols, and are not necessarily to be interpreted as literal numbers. But the picture is clear. The bear has an insatiable desire to devour, and this was most certainly a feature of the Medo-Persian Empire at the time of the vision. It was hungry for conquest. If the three ribs refer to anything at all, they must be the three empires which were conquered by Medo-Persia — namely Babylon, Lydia and Egypt.

Daniel has thus seen two consecutive world empires. As he watches, he sees a third. Another beast emerges from the ocean. 'After this I beheld, and lo another, like a leopard (or panther), which had upon the back of it four wings of a fowl; the beast had also four heads; and dominion was given to it' (6).

We are confronted with a panther with four wings! Such things happen in dreams. It is twice as swift as the lion which emerged first. Its four wings are matched by four heads.

In biblical symbolism the number four speaks of the world. The way that the Scriptures speak of the four winds, and the four corners of the earth, bears this out. What we have before us now is a kingdom which conquers swiftly, and which conquers the world. This is a reference to the rapid expansion of the Greek Empire under Alexander the Great. As we would expect, the third beast corresponds to the third empire of Nebuchadnezzar's vision in chapter 2. First of all, we have had Babylon, then Medo-Persia and now swift-conquering Greece.

What about the fourth beast which is described in verse 7? Is it a lion? Is it a bear? Is it a panther? It is none of them. But what it is we cannot say; it is indescribable.

This monster rampages, conquers, crushes and stamps. It is totally different from anything which has gone before. But the reference to iron shows clearly that this fourth beast is identical with the fourth section of the image mentioned in chapter 2. It is the great empire of Rome. We have the same kingdoms as before, and in the same order. The last of them is spiteful Rome.

We must not forget that everything recorded in this chapter is a prophet's dream. All of its details are symbols. We must be careful to keep this in mind as we study what happens next. Daniel sees three phases in the history of the fourth beast. At the end of verse 7, and in verse 8, he sees the beast itself. It is only after his attention has been drawn to its stupendous strength and its crushing power that we are told about its ten horns.

These ten horns represent a later stage in the history of this empire. We know that because verse 24 specifically tells us that these ten horns came *out* of this kingdom.

In the Bible the horn is a symbol of power. Ten is almost certainly a symbolic number. It is hard to see how we can insist that it be taken literally when all the other recorded details of the vision are evidently not to be taken that way.

Please disagree with the interpretation that follows, if you like. But please do not disagree with the important lesson that we are going to learn from it.

As I understand it, the vision is predicting that in direct succession to the Roman Empire, and springing out of it, will be a multiplicity of kingdoms. None of these could have arisen without Rome, and yet none of them *is* Rome. For example, modern Europe as we know it owes it existence to Rome, and yet is not a continuation of the Roman Empire. The vision teaches that a multiplicity of dominions will spring out of Rome. Ten stands simply for completeness, and should not be pressed. It is a round number. Those who insist on interpreting it literally are in an awful difficulty. They have no hope of identifying the kingdoms involved, because God's Word does not give to us the remotest clue as to who they may be. Such interpreters are left to the mercy of their own speculations, and must resort to guesswork. We consider that we are on safer ground when we claim nothing more than that a multiplicity of political powers will follow in the wake of Rome and owe something to it.

But after Rome, and the ten ensuing kingdoms, comes a third stage of history. It is the period of the little horn which is referred to in verse 8. This little horn is an eleventh horn. Verse 24 dogmatically tells us that it follows the others. It arises from among the others, displaces some of them, and holds sway.

In this eleventh kingdom power is concentrated in an individual. You might be forgiven if you were to think that this individual is supernatural. But he is not. That is why it is emphasized that he has the eyes of a man.

This chapter is predicting that a powerful figure will arise who appears to be supernatural, but who, in fact, is only a man. He speaks 'great things' (8). In the Bible this expression consistently refers to blasphemy, arrogant words and puffed-up statements. At this stage in the vision all thought of the fourth beast is lost, and our whole attention is focused on this little horn.

I am convinced in my own mind that this little horn is the same individual as is referred to in 2 Thessalonians 2, verses 3 and 4. He is 'the son of perdition; who opposeth and exalteth himself above all that is called God, or that is worshipped; so that he as God sitteth in the temple of God, shewing himself that he is God'.

What we have in Daniel 7 is a survey of human history from

the time of Daniel to the very end of the world. Four great kingdoms will arise, one after the other. These will be followed by a multiplicity of kingdoms springing from the fourth. At the end, power will be concentrated in a single blasphemous individual. Although only a man, he will appear to be supernatural, and will be the enemy of God and what is godly.

While Daniel saw all this, he also saw something else, as we learn from verses 9 to 14. We shall be the poorest of people if we spend all our time thinking about the beasts and the horns, and fail to see the other things that were revealed to the prophet that night.

The little horn speaks its arrogant blasphemies, but while it does so Daniel lifts up his eyes to heaven. There he sees a succession of thrones set up. Lesser thrones surround one great throne. On that central throne he sees (in symbol) the eternal God in His majesty, the One who is worthy of all veneration and worship. It is a vivid picture of purity and dignity that we have before us. God is on His throne, and His throne is a fiery chariot. It is a vision which thrills the heart of every believer. World history is going its way but, reigning over it all, with His throne unaffected by earthly events, is the great God.

Streaming from that throne is power to put down all that opposes Him (10). God is the great Invincible. Surrounded by countless glorious creatures, He presides over His court of judgement. Books are there which record the actions of every man and woman; and the books are open.

This is as much part of Daniel's vision as the beasts and the horns. Daniel watches until he sees that by a mere decision of the heavenly King that last beast, and all that comes from it, is finished (11). No war is necessary to bring this to pass. A word is sufficient. The divine sentence ends it all. A word from the King — and the beast is no more. Only One is omnipotent, and that is God. That is the heart of the vision.

The divine court is not an afterthought which appears, just in time, at the end of history. It is sitting all the time. If we forget this, we are likely to misunderstand verse 12. The court is not only responsible for the final overthrow of evil. All the other empires, too, ended as a result of its decision. None of them had an ending as dramatic as the final one. However, they all, without exception, lost their power to rule because of a divine decree, although they were allowed to continue for a determined time in some form afterwards.

But even verse 12 is not the end of the vision. In verse 13 Daniel also saw something else.

Into that heavenly court comes a human form — a human form that has all the honour and dignity of the Deity! Ushered in to have a divine audience is one *'like* the Son of man'. It cannot possibly be any other than our Lord Jesus Christ. The word 'like' is used because He had not yet clothed Himself in our human nature, and so, even in a vision, the Scripture is careful to point out that His appearance was only a foreshadowing of what He was later to be. He was not *yet* a man. He only appeared as one. At the time of the vision His real humanity lay in the future.

We remember that our Lord often referred to Himself as 'the Son of Man', and especially when He was laying claim to deity. By using that expression He was deliberately reminding us of the reality of His human nature, while at the same time identifying Himself as the One with divine honours referred to in Daniel 7.

It is to this Christ that an eternal kingdom is given! Notice how this is stressed, both positively and negatively, in verse 14: 'And there was given him dominion, and glory, and a kingdom, that all people, nations, and languages, should serve him: his dominion is an everlasting dominion, which shall not pass away, and his kingdom that which shall not be destroyed.'

What a great vision Daniel had that night! World empires rise, and prosper and disappear. One last empire is perpetuated in some form almost to the end of the world. This is followed by the arising of Antichrist — a blasphemous individual who looks as if he will reign for ever. But one word from God's heavenly court finishes him. This court, which brings all human reign to an end, grants to one Person the privilege of reigning for ever. It is the Lord Jesus Christ. When all human kingdoms have gone, the Man who is God will still be reigning! Every other kingdom is doomed to fall by God's decree, but of *His* kingdom there shall be no end. Every knee shall bow to Him, and every tongue confess that *Jesus Christ is Lord*!

That is what Daniel saw.

Daniel 7 99

How it was interpreted

The vision which Daniel saw troubled him (15). It made him anxious. So he turned to one of the heavenly attendants and asked for it to be explained (16).

He was told plainly that the four beasts represent four empires, or 'kings', and that the only people who will ever experience an eternal kingdom are the people of God (17-18).

Obviously no earthly kingdom is being spoken of, because no such kingdom could possibly be described as everlasting. We can forget the idea of an earthly 'millennium'. The everlasting kingdom which Daniel saw is obviously the kingdom of God which is established in our hearts when we believe the gospel, the consummation of which we shall eternally enjoy in glory.

From verses 19 to 22 it is clear that the fourth beast was of particular interest to Daniel. In this section we are given the additional detail that it had claws of brass. But the little horn was of greater interest still. An additional detail is given concerning this, too. We are told that it became bigger than any of the ten horns which preceded it (20). Its power is unprecedented. The individual whom it represents is the unrivalled opponent of the Lord's people, who breaks forth into evil as nobody has ever done before him. He uses his power in such a way that the people of God are unable to stand before him. His days appear as the apparent and ultimate triumph of evil over all that is good and godly (21). This is the way that things will look until he is put down by the Ancient of Days, who will at last welcome His people into a kingdom that is safe, secure and eternal.

The interpretation of the vision traces the might of Rome — mightier in its conquests than anything before it (23). We stress again that it is from this beast that the following multiplicity of kingdoms sprang. It gave way to them, and was succeeded by them. It is important to note this, for one often hears talk about the possibility of a revived Roman Empire, with Daniel 7 being quoted in support of the idea. There is not the slightest suggestion in this chapter that the Roman Empire will be revived. In fact the passage seems to be teaching the very opposite. Rome will give way to ten ensuing kingdoms, which in turn will eventually be succeeded by the little horn, with all its aggression and presumption (24). This will put down three of the previous kings, but we are given no clue as to how or when this is to happen, or precisely what it means. Once more we express our doubt as to whether the number three is to be taken literally.

The whole of history is moving towards the emergence of the little horn, and the time of his blasphemy, and his persecution of the Lord's people (25). He will even be arrogant enough to change times and seasons ordained by God Himself. Those will be terrible days — days when the Lord's people will be in his hands!

For how long will he exercise this unchallenged power? The end of verse 25 gives us the answer: '... until a time and times and the dividing of time'.

How long is that? Once more I must ask you to disagree with me if you wish, but to me the interpretation which follows seems reasonable, and I believe that it is right. This awful individual will come on to the scene, and will for a time persecute God's people and have his evil way. When that time is over, he will do it for *twice* that time. Then it will look as if he is going to continue for twice *that* time. It will appear as if he is to be here for ever, and as if there will never be an end to the unrestrained evil of his reign. However, instead of that his period of rule will be time, times — and half a time! God will cut him short. He will ruin him while his evil power is in full flow, and when he is at the very height of his power. Wonderful! Marvellous! That interpretation is a lot better than understanding the riddle of the times to mean three and a half! Disagree with whom you please on this point. Whatever may be the details of your own interpretation, the central teaching of verse 25 remains unchanged. The day will come when Antichrist's time will be up! He will not go on for ever, however permanent he may seem. There will be a halt.

And who will call the halt? Verse 26 tells us. The court of heaven will remove both him and all his power. Evil may appear omnipotent, but it is an illusion. Absolute power belongs to God alone, and the doom of evil is therefore a certainty. 'The judgment shall sit, and they shall take away his dominion, to consume and to destroy it unto the end' (26).

Evil is removed from the globe by a word — a word from God! The culmination of history will not be the triumph of evil,

Daniel 7

but the triumph of the Lord's people (27). Those whom this evil person will have oppressed will no longer be the tail, but the head, and will be untroubled and eternally secure in an everlasting kingdom of righteousness. The time is coming when we shall look around for the wicked and ungodly, and for all wicked powers, and they will be gone!

This is what Daniel saw, and how it was interpreted. It shook him! (28.) It filled him with turmoil, both visibly and inwardly. It is terrific truth, in the full sense of that term. The good prophet hid it in his heart, and made it part of his armoury. So should we.

What it means to us

Daniel 7 means that we are no longer in the dark about the future history of the world. Towards the close of this present age the little horn will appear. The 'man of sin' will wage war on God's people. He will become stronger and stronger, and they will be unable to stand against him. We envisage that organized missionary activity will be crushed, and that the church of God will be broken, destroyed and ruined. Its visible form will disappear.

There will still be Christians, for we have repeatedly learned that nothing can destroy God's remnant. But as far as the godless world is concerned, all traces of God, His worship and His people, will be gone. It will look as if evil has won the day. It will seem as if Satan has triumphed. There will be such an unloosing of ungodly forces that it will appear as if God has abdicated His throne.

It is *at that moment* that the power of evil will be cut off. The Lord Jesus Christ shall suddenly return from heaven. He will take home His people to eternally reign with Him. There will be no trace of evil in the new heaven and the new earth, while all who have loved and cherished a lie will suffer justly, and eternally, in hell.

That is a matter for us, like Daniel, to keep constantly in our hearts.

Meanwhile we ought to prepare ourselves for the rough ride ahead. This would be true if this chapter were the only passage in God's Word which spoke of these things. But it is not. We have seen how the same teaching is given by Paul in 2 Thessalonians. Even a superficial reading of Revelation underlines the same truth. Dark days await the church of Christ. Evil men will wax worse and worse. Eventually the 'man of sin' will be revealed, and the light will go out. There cannot be a second advent of our Lord until this awful figure has appeared (2 Thessalonians 2:1-12).

Yet at that time God will be as much in control as ever! Nothing will have happened other than what He predicted. His control of history is absolute, even when He seems to be absent from the world He has made.

In those days it will appear as if evil has become a permanent fixture. *That* will be the moment of God's momentous display of justice and power. He will end the world and summon every evildoer to His judgement. We shall search for the blasphemer, the persecutor, the merchant of pornography, and every breaker of the Ten Commandments — and will find that every one has entered into his deserved condemnation.

All rule will be seen to be in the hands of One who bears the marks of whipping, of a crown of thorns, of crucifixion and of piercing. The title of 'Lord' will be exclusively His. Those who have loved Him and submitted to Him by repenting and believing the gospel will share His glory. They will rejoice in the fathomless wonder of being eternally with Him as citizens of the kingdom which shall never pass away.

Is it worth remaining true to God in a hostile environment? Is it worth putting up with the contempt and cruelty of the world around in order to identify with a persecuted minority?

Did Daniel ask that question? Do you? The dream that God gave him was the answer that he needed, and is enough for our needs, too. Does it really matter if we do not understand all its details? The overall message is so clear that we can never again want to side with the majority. It is not worth it. The future does not belong to them, but to us. We can dare to stand alone.

10.
THE LITTLE HORN

Please read Daniel chapter 8

Daniel has already had two glimpses into the future, and in this chapter he has a third. There was some overlap between the interpretation of Nebuchadnezzar's dream in chapter 2 and his dream of the four beasts from the sea in our last chapter. Both spoke of four coming world empires. The vision of chapter 8 also has some overlap with these previous visions, but contains a good deal of new information, too. With its opening verse the book of Daniel returns from the Aramaic, in which everything since 2:4 has been written, to Hebrew.

The two previous visions took place while Babylon was still standing, and that is also the case with this one. It occurred before the fingers of a man's hand announced Belshazzar's doom, in the third year of his reign (1).

Both the previous visions were night visions. They were dreams; but not this one. This took place in the daytime, while Daniel was conscious (2,27). If he was not conscious while he received the vision, how could he have lost consciousness at its end?

He was caught up in the Spirit, but he was not asleep. He was not 'day-dreaming', in the sense in which we use that expression today. It was a spiritual vision given during the daytime. It was similar in some respects to what had gone before, which is why Daniel speaks of it as he does at the end of verse 1: '... after that which appeared unto me at the first'.

Daniel was transported in the Spirit to Susa — the city which, after the collapse of Babylon, was to become the capital of the Persian Empire. He sat down beside the Ulai, which was in fact a large artificial canal, nine hundred feet wide, and which connected two prominent rivers so that the craft which navigated them could pass from one to the other. It was there that he had the vision which we now come to study.

What Daniel saw and heard

What Daniel saw and heard is recorded for us in verses 3 to 14.

Spiritually seated by the river, he lifted up his eyes. He saw a ram which had two horns and, as he watched, one of its horns became larger than the other. The two horns were quite large, but it was the one which appeared later which became the bigger.

The ram with its two horns symbolizes the empire of the Medes and the Persians. There can be no speculation about this, because this is what we are plainly told in verse 20: 'The ram which thou sawest having two horns are the kings of Media and Persia.'

In history these nations were to form one empire and to bring about the fall of Babylon. At first, the Medes had the upper hand, and it was one of their number who was the first ruler of the combined empire. This was Darius, as we have already learned. But this situation did not last long. Very soon the Persians became dominant and Cyrus ascended the imperial throne. The symbol of Persia was a ram, and the Persian king carried the image of one in front of him whenever he went into battle. We are not therefore surprised to find that in Daniel's vision a ram is the symbol of the Medo-Persian empire.

It is a characteristic of rams to be aggressive, and to butt. As Daniel watched the ram before him, he saw it pushing and butting in every direction except east (4). It is a historical fact that the Medes and Persians made many great military conquests, especially under Cyrus. In the last vision their empire was addressed with the words, 'Arise, devour much flesh' (7:5). But they did not manage to gain much territory in the east, and what they did conquer there they very soon lost. What Daniel saw in a predictive vision was exactly matched by the historical events which later followed.

But now the dream changes (5). Racing in from the west — so fast that its feet do not touch the ground — is a male goat. It has one horn, which is in the centre of its head.

What is this 'he goat ... from the west on the face of the whole earth'? It is the Greek Empire; verse 21 tells us so. The horn is its 'first king' (21), namely Alexander the Great. The feet not touching the ground signify the rapidity of Alexander's

Daniel 8

conquests, while the expression 'the face of the whole earth' speaks of their enormity.

Daniel watches, and sees the he-goat collide with the ram! (6.) With its head down and its horn forward, the enraged and rushing goat hits the ram, turns on it with devouring fury and strikes it down. The ram is totally humiliated. Its two horns are broken, its resistance crushed, and its fallen body trampled on. There is no escape and no rescue. It is a prediction of the complete subjugation and defeat of the Medo-Persian Empire by the Greeks.

We next read that 'The he-goat waxed very great' (8). Puffed up by the speed and number of his conquests, Alexander the Great inevitably became inflated with pride. But his arrogance was short-lived. At the very height of his power he was struck down: 'And when he was strong, the great horn was broken.' The verse does not mention precisely who did the striking, because it was the unseen hand of God. He merely stretched out and snapped the great horn, and it was broken for ever.

Alexander was replaced by four others (8). The Greek Empire continued after his death. The he-goat did not die when he did. Immediately after his death the empire split into five, but almost straight after that it settled down into four distinct quarters. Macedonia was under Cassander, Thrace and Asia Minor under Lysimachus, Syria under Seleucus and Egypt under Ptolemy. Instead of the great horn there were four notable ones, but not one of them was as great as the original horn. Once more nothing happened other than what the Scriptures had predicted. What others saw only after the event, Daniel saw in prophetic vision beforehand.

Daniel's attention is now on the four horns, and he notices that 'Out of one of them came forth a little horn' (9). From a small beginning it grew to great power, and its power stretched south and east, and then into 'the pleasant land' — into the promised land of Canaan.

There can be no doubt that verse 9 refers to the rise of a man known to us in history as Antiochus Epiphanes. As predicted, he came from one of the distinct quarters of the Greek empire. Antiochus arose from the Seleucid quarter and soon afterwards spoiled Egypt with an immense army. He next turned his attention eastwards and took Elymais and Armenia. After this he invaded Canaan. It is this man who is the little horn of this chapter.

From the Seleucids arose this great persecutor of the people of God. The Jewish historian, Josephus, was later to write of him, 'And there would arise from their number a certain king who would make war on the Jewish nation and their laws, deprive them of the form of government based on these laws, spoil the temple and prevent the sacrifices from being offered for three years. And these misfortunes our nation did in fact come to experience under Antiochus Epiphanes, just as Daniel many years before saw and wrote that they would happen.'

This little horn 'waxed great, even to the host of heaven; and it cast down some of the host and of the stars to the ground, and stamped upon them' (10).

What does that mean? We understand it better when we remember that in Exodus 7:4 and 12:41 the tribes of Israel are called the hosts of the Lord. It is not a reference to the angels, but to Antiochus' crimes against the people of the Lord, whom he cruelly crushed. To persecute them is to sin against heaven. This is well illustrated by Jesus' words from heaven to Saul of Tarsus, who up until then had been the enemy of God's people: 'Saul, Saul, why persecutest thou *me*?' (Acts 9:4.)

But that was not the end of Antiochus' blasphemous action. The remainder of his career is perfectly predicted in verses 11 and 12. He actually defied God, 'the prince of the host'. He took away all the regular temple services, and although he did not actually destroy the temple's structure, he desecrated it to such an extent that it became impossible to use it. All this was recorded, before it took place, in verse 11 of our chapter.

What does verse 12 mean? If we are using the Authorized Version we will understand it better by taking out the word 'against', and replacing it with the phrase 'along with'. The verse now makes perfect sense to a modern reader. Just as the daily sacrifices were given into Antiochus' hand, and he desecrated them — in the same way an enormous number of the tribes of Israel were given into his hand, and he did with them exactly as he pleased. It was a time in Israel's history when truth was cast to the ground, and this evil man practised evil without restraint and prospered in it. It was a period of unthinkable suffering for the people of God. All was darkness, and there seemed to be no light at all.

This was the vision Daniel saw and, as he saw it, he heard a

Daniel 8

'saint' speaking — that is 'a holy one', an angel (13).

It seems that the angel was recounting to another angel the very events which Daniel was seeing in his vision. The response of the second angel was to ask, 'How long will this appalling state of affairs go on? How long will that awful man have power over the people of God? How long will Antiochus Epiphanes be able to proceed with his transgressions, blasphemy and persecution?'

The answer that was given is recorded in verse 14: 'Unto two thousand and three hundred days; 'then shall the sanctuary be cleansed'.

If we consider a year to be three hundred and sixty days — and most scholars agree that it is wise to do this when dealing with biblical numbers — we find that this figure comes to about six years and four months. This figure ties up with what transpired. From 171 to 165 B.C. Antiochus Epiphanes persecuted the Jews and continued with his abominations. During the last three and a half years of that period the temple was used for heathen sacrifices. The Maccabean revolt permitted the temple to be reconsecrated and reopened for the worship of Jehovah, and shortly afterwards Antiochus died. The promise at the end of verse 14 came true. It all happened just as Daniel had previously seen and heard.

What all this meant

We have already seen what all this meant. The divine interpretation of the vision is given in verses 15 to the end of the chapter, and we have referred to it as we have gone along. But there are some details of which we have not yet taken note, and we come to those now. At the same time we shall underline some of the points that we have already made.

When he had received the vision, Daniel 'sought for the meaning' (15). As he did so there stood before him one who was not a man, but had a man's appearance. This is a common way of describing an angel in the Bible, and it soon becomes obvious that this is what the visitor was.

The next thing was that Daniel heard a human voice giving instructions to this angel (16). John Calvin was right to remind us that this voice could not possibly belong to any other than our Lord Jesus Christ. Who else can command the angels? And who else can do it with a human voice (a further pledge of His coming incarnation)? 'Gabriel,' He says, 'Make this man to understand the vision.'

There are two angels who are named in the Bible. Gabriel, mentioned here, means 'man of God'. The other is the archangel Michael, and we shall read of him in 10:13.

In obedience to Christ's command Gabriel approaches Daniel (17). The prophet is filled with terror, because he is a sinner in the presence of sinlessness. He falls on his face, as any of us would do in a similar situation. He is not in the presence of God, but to be in the presence of His holy messenger is enough to overwhelm him with a sense of unworthiness. But Daniel's feeling of intimidation does not stop the angel speaking. He calls him 'son of man' to stress the prophet's weakness and to prepare him for the divine interpretation of the vision which is about to be given.

'Understand, O son of man: for at the time of the end shall be the vision' (17).

This cannot possibly be a reference to the end of the world, because the identification of the little horn as Antiochus Epiphanes is too obvious to be missed. The vision is about the days of the Greek persecutor, not the end of the world. What then can Gabriel be referring to? Only one answer is possible. He must be talking about the end of those special troubles which were to come upon the Jews before the time of the Messianic kingdom.

The experience of being addressed by an angel proves to be too much for Daniel. It is so overwhelming and so intimidating that he loses consciousness (18). He has to be touched by Gabriel, and helped to his feet before the interpretation can continue.

Gabriel's next words confirm the interpretation we have given of the end of verse 17 'Behold, I will make thee know what shall be in the last end of the indignation: for at the time appointed the end shall be' (19).

In other words, the vision is going to take place at the latter end of God's present indignation with the Jews, and will occur because God has appointed that it will do so. That is what the angel said. Those who relegate the fulfilment of the vision to the very end of the world have chosen their own theories in

Daniel 8

preference to an angel's words.

It is hard to see how anybody can miss what the vision means. The ram is specifically said to be Medo-Persia (20). The he-goat is plainly identified as the Greek Empire, and the horn as its first king — which must be Alexander the Great (21). The four ensuing horns are dogmatically said to be the splitting up of the Greek empire, though not with the strength of that first king (22). It is towards the end of *their* dominion that the little horn will emerge (23). To consider that the vision is about the end of the world is not only a flight of fancy, it is also to fly in the face of a divinely given interpretation which has come by the mouth of an angel. Many modern prophetic interpretations of this chapter are outspoken contradictions of heaven.

Let us ponder the description of the coming Antiochus Epiphanes which is given to us in verses 23 to 25. He is described as 'a king of fierce countenance'. And he was. He strutted on to the pages of history as a hard, determined, unyielding and adamant man.

He is also said to be 'understanding dark sentences' — a reference to the fact that Antiochus was a man who practised deceit, although he was hard to deceive.

'And his power shall be mighty, but not by his own power' (24). Antiochus was to have great attainments, but they would not be attributable simply to his own cunning. He could have had nothing without the providence of God.

'And he shall destroy wonderfully, and shall prosper, and practise, and shall destroy the mighty and the holy people.' This was a prediction that he would destroy to a remarkable degree and go from strength to strength in his wickedness. He put down all his rivals, and then turned his venom on the Old Testament Jew and upon those who were the divine remnant, who loved the coming Christ.

'And through his policy also he shall cause craft to prosper in his hand' (25). It was a time when deceit flourished in the land. '... And he shall magnify himself in his heart.' He did. As his reign proceeded he became increasingly inflated with a sense of his own self-importance. '... And by peace shall destroy many.' This exactly described Antiochus' most common tactic. He was friendly with many people and, when their defences were down and they no longer felt the need to be on their guard, he cut them down. '... He shall also stand up against the Prince of princes.' Once more it is predicted that this coming little horn will be outspoken against God. This was to be the most obvious feature of Antiochus' reign of terror.

We need, however, to take note of the end of verse 25: '... But he shall be broken without hand.'

It was a stone cut out 'without hands' that destroyed the image of Nebuchadnezzar's dream (2:34). It was fingers without a hand that announced Belshazzar's doom (5:5). The hand of God is an unseen hand. The same hand is to be responsible for the downfall of Antiochus. However great the tyrant, it requires nothing more than the mere sweep of God's invisible hand to remove him from the stage of history!

'You have heard the truth, Daniel,' says the angel (26). 'Now preserve the vision, because the future will need a record of what you have seen.'

And it did. In those darkest of days, when the people of God were being hounded and killed in the days of Antiochus Epiphanes, they needed and they had the comfort of this chapter of Daniel. Throughout that period they were consoled by knowing that this wicked man could not have stepped on to the page of history without divine permission and that everything he did, however awful, was nothing other than what God had predicted centuries earlier. They knew that in God's time, and in fulfilment of verse 25, he would at last be removed. To know all this was an indescribable comfort to them in horrific times.

That was the effect of this vision on future days. But what was its effect on the man who first received it? Verse 27 tells us. Daniel found it all so overwhelming that for a while he was too ill to serve the king. He could not go back to work. Even when he did, the impression that the vision left on his mind was indelible. It continued to perplex him and was beyond the understanding of all who heard of it. Daniel could not greet the revelation of a forthcoming unloosing of evil with indifference.

What it means for us

We should not leave this chapter without deriving some lessons from it ourselves.

We can learn one from the fact that the coming Antiochus

Epiphanes is here described as 'a little horn' (9). In the previous chapter we read of another little horn — an individual who will come at the end of time and who will cause the Lord's people to suffer as they have never done before. No doubt we find it hard to believe that the coming of such a person is a fact and that he will be as easily removed as we have learned.

But the chapter we are now studying speaks of Antiochus as a little horn. He came exactly as it was written of him and was removed as easily as was predicted. Those who first heard the prophecies regarding him almost certainly found them hard to believe. This did not stop them happening. The future events for which *we* wait are equally certain and we should live in the light of them. The certainty of Antichrist's coming should make us serious. The certainty of his removal should make us rejoice!

But why are both Antiochus, at the end of the second century B.C., and the man of sin, at the end of the world, described as little horns? They are distinct and different individuals. One has already come, and one has yet to come. Why should they be described in identical terms?

This is because, in a very real sense, they are one and the same thing. The New Testament sheds light on this point. It tells us of the coming of a personal Antichrist, as we have seen. Yet it also tells us that the spirit of antichrist is already in the world, and that many antichrists have already come (1 John 2: 18-19; 4:3; 2 John 1:7). The previous antichrists are given the same title as the final one because they are his precursors. He will be greater in power and infinitely more wicked. But he will not be different in *type* from those whose who have preceded him. He will be all that they were, but *to a greater degree*. His coming will not introduce into the world something it has never experienced before. It will be what it has already witnessed a thousand times, but with much more *intensity*.

There will have been many little horns before the final one. Antiochus Epiphanes was one. There have been countless others who have defied God and turned with venom on His people, determining to crush them out of existence. Think of Nero, an almost uncountable number of popes, of Hitler, of Khruschev, of Mao Tse Tung and of Haxhi Lleshi, last communist president of Albania. These are all examples of little horns.

But to God, we must remember, they are all *little* horns. To us their power is impressive, but not one of them is great in His eyes. Their arrogance may ring with confidence. They may have a look of permanence. To God this means nothing. He has contempt for mortal power. He removes them as He pleases, and will remove the final Antichrist with the same omnipotent ease. He sweeps away each one in the succession when He wishes, and the only difference about the final one will be that he is last in the queue.

How God laughs at human power! To Him the great Medo-Persian Empire is nothing more than a lop-sided ram. The might of Greece is a woolly sheep, and Alexander the Great a brittle horn that can be snapped with the fingers!

But what about Antiochus Epiphanes? His kingdom was never really very large, but was of more significance to God because its ruler spat in the face of heaven. This is why so much space is devoted to him in this book, compared with the world empires which are mentioned. God does not measure the importance of world events as we do. The relative importance of an incident, or a regime, is measured by the effect that it has on His people. After all, they are the apple of His eye. Antiochus turned on them in a way the greater empires did not. The world's history books give very little attention to his activities, although they write volumes about Persia and Rome. But not so God. He notes the details of all that he does, and pledges to His people that 'he shall be broken without hand'. The world does not give much thought to their fortunes. The infinite God does. He *cares* for His own.

How great God is! How is it that He can reveal future history to His prophet, centuries before it happens? It is because He is the God of history, and because all events everywhere serve His sovereign will. What a comfort to know that no evil power can arise without His express decree! How consoling to be aware that He who rules history has guaranteed that His Son shall finally triumph over all rule and authority, and that every display of evil will at last be put down! What folly it is to fight against such a God! What wisdom it is to walk with Him! What convincing power is in the argument: 'If God be for us, who can be against us?'! (Romans 8:31.)

Daniel 8

The angel Gabriel from God

There is another point that we should notice before we leave this chapter. In it we read of the angel Gabriel bringing to earth a message from God. We should remember that this is not the only time that he did this.

When the birth of John the Baptist was to be announced, Gabriel came to his father: 'And the angel answering said unto him, I am Gabriel, that stand in the presence of God; and am sent to speak unto thee, and to shew thee these glad tidings' (Luke 1:19). And so Zacharias met Gabriel.

In the sixth month of Elisabeth's pregnancy, 'The angel Gabriel was sent from God unto a city of Galilee, named Nazareth, to a virgin espoused to a man whose name was Joseph, of the house of David; and the virgin's name was Mary' (Luke 1:26-27).

The holy angel announced the birth of two babies! When the first was born, his father burst into praise, and spoke about the coming Christ who was shortly to be born of Mary, saying, 'Blessed be the Lord God of Israel; for he hath visited and redeemed his people, and hath raised up an horn of salvation for us in the house of his servant David' (Luke 1:68-69).

In Daniel chapter 8 we have read of several horns — a horn outgrowing another, a horn broken, four horns which followed and a little horn which rose from one of the four. But the man to whom Gabriel gave a message here speaks of *another* horn!

In the Scriptures, as we have seen, the horn is a symbol of princely power. Our chapter has told us of many such displays of human power which have come and gone. But at the coming of Christ Zacharias' song assures us that at last *God* has given us a horn. A horn of God's own making is coming into the world.

He is telling us that every other rule and dominion is bound to fail. But God has a horn. God has One who will rule and reign. It is a further underlining of one of the main themes of the book of Daniel. There is no enduring dominion except that of the Lord Jesus Christ!

Not a ram nor a goat, but a Lamb

When Zacharias' son grew up and began his ministry as the forerunner of the promised Messiah, how did he announce Him? 'Behold the Lamb of God ...' (John 1:29).

When the apostle John was given the privilege of seeing a symbolic vision of heaven, what did he see bearing rule there? Was it a ram, or a he-goat? He saw a lion — a lion described as 'a Lamb as it had been slain' (Revelation 5:5-6).

When all other horns have come and gone, God *still* has a horn! When rams and he-goats have crossed the stage of history, God has a Lamb! And all heaven says, 'Worthy is the Lamb that was slain to receive power, and riches, and wisdom, and strength, and honour, and glory, and blessing. And every creature which is in heaven, and on the earth, and under the earth, and such as are in the sea, and all that are in them, heard I saying, Blessing, and honour, and glory, and power, be unto him that sitteth upon the throne, and unto the Lamb for ever and ever' (Revelation 5:12-13).

Our minds cannot help leaping from Daniel chapter 8 to these other references. One is suggestive of the others, especially because the powers mentioned in our chapter are so obviously *passing* powers. We enquire where lasting rule and dominion are to be found, and remember at once what God has declared concerning the Lamb, the Horn of our salvation.

This is why we can unashamedly take Christ's side at our places of work or study, even though we may be alone in doing so. If all our relatives or neighbours should ignore or reject Him, we can still boldly identify with Him. All other power is passing. No kingdom except His will prevail. All that harms His people will come to nothing, but they themselves will never be forgotten. It is armed by such assurances that we can

> Dare to be a Daniel!
> Dare to stand alone!
> Dare to have a purpose firm!
> Dare to make it known.

11.
A GREAT PRAYER

Please read Daniel chapter 9

This chapter records a great discovery, a great prayer and a great revelation. Some have regarded it as a controversial chapter, but it must surely be one of the most exciting sections in the whole of the book of Daniel.

A great discovery

The great discovery is recorded in the opening two verses. To understand it fully we must remember the events of chapter 1. They took place in 605 B.C. In that year Nebuchadnezzar had captured Jerusalem and had taken Daniel and a vast number of others into exile. The majority of the nation had then followed at intervals afterwards. All that was sixty-eight years ago. Daniel had been in Babylon nearly seventy years.

In this chapter Daniel is now an old man. He was fourteen when he had been taken captive, so is now eighty-two years old. It is 537 B.C., the first year of Darius the Mede. The elderly prophet can look back over sixty-eight years of standing valiantly for the Lord. In all those years, with just a handful of others, he has stood alone for God and has not compromised on any occasion with the temptation to be unfaithful to his Lord.

And now the Babylonian Empire has fallen, just as his God-given visions had predicted. Medo-Persia rules the world and Darius the Mede rules Medo-Persia. As for Daniel, as we saw in chapter 6, he has risen to unprecedented heights of importance. In the new regime he is second only to the king himself.

Many years have passed since he last saw Jerusalem, but the old man's faith is as fresh as ever. Trials have not broken it.

Promotion has not eroded it or seduced him to love other things more than his God. So as the chapter opens we find him reading his Bible. It would not have been a single volume like our printed Bibles today, but a collection of scrolls, or 'books', as it is translated in many versions.

Daniel was a great prophet and had had many remarkable visions and revelations, but he never outgrew the need to read his Bible. His example is worth noting.

On this particular occasion he is reading from the scrolls of Jeremiah. When he was a boy back in Jerusalem he had probably heard Jeremiah in person. He certainly would have known of him. Jeremiah's prophecies had been written down and, because they were the Word of God, had been wonderfully preserved in the following years. It was these that Daniel was reading. As he did so, he could hardly believe his eyes ...!

As he read, Daniel came to see something he had never seen before. What was it? To find out, we must turn to Jeremiah 25:8-11 and 29:10-14.

In Jeremiah 25 the prophet's eyes would have rested on the following words: 'Therefore thus saith the Lord of hosts; Because ye have not heard my words, behold, I will send and take all the families of the north, saith the Lord, and Nebuchadnezzar the king of Babylon, my servant, and will bring them against this land, and against the inhabitants thereof, and against all these nations round about, and will utterly destroy them, and make them an astonishment, and an hissing, and perpetual desolations' (Jeremiah 25:8-9).

The old man would have reflected how very true Jeremiah's predictions had been. From the moment of Nebuchadnezzar's arrival the land had indeed been such a desolation.

He would have read on: 'Moreover I will take from them the voice of mirth, and the voice of gladness, the voice of the bridegroom, and the voice of the bride, the sound of the millstones, and the light of the candle' (Jeremiah 25:10).

This would have caused him to ponder, too. Many young people, ready to marry, had been suddenly separated by the captivity. The land had been filled with depression and with many tears.

But then he read this: 'And this whole land shall be a desolation, and an astonishment; and these nations shall serve the king of Babylon *seventy years*' (Jeremiah 25:11).

Babylon was gone, but the man now ruling the Medo-Persian Empire was ruling the territory which had once been the Babylonian Empire. The change of government had not affected the fact that the Jews were still in exile far from home. Daniel himself had been there from the beginning, sixty-eight years earlier. But he was now reading that the duration of the exile was to be but two years more!

So he read on, and before long came to Jeremiah 29:10-14: 'For thus saith the Lord, That after seventy years be accomplished at Babylon I will visit you, and perform my good word toward you, in causing you to return to this place. For I know the thoughts that I think toward you, saith the Lord, thoughts of peace, and not of evil, to give you an expected end. Then shall ye call upon me, and ye shall go and pray unto me, and I will hearken unto you. And ye shall seek me, and find me, when ye shall search for me with all your heart. And I will be found of you, saith the Lord: and I will turn away your captivity, and I will gather you from all the nations, and from all the places whither I have driven you, saith the Lord; and I will bring you again into the place whence I caused you to be carried away captive.'

There it was again! In the Scriptures in front of him Daniel once more read a divine promise that the exile would end after seventy years. If God's people returned to Him, they would be restored to their land.

We can imagine the old man's heart beginning to leap and dance. Jerusalem to him was only a boyhood memory, but he had never forgotten it, and had never lost the desire to go back there. For sixty-eight years he had prayed towards it, with his windows open. Everything inside him had been longing to return. And now he found himself reading a divine promise that after seventy years God's people can go back to that home!

How excited he must have been as he counted out the years. The time was almost ripe. And yet there was no visible sign that the promise could possibly be fulfilled. The new empire had not given any indication whatever that it would be willing to release the captive Jews. Nor was there any sign that the exiled people were about to return to their offended Lord with the whole of their heart. It was true that they had given up idolatry, which had been the prime cause of the exile. But that was all.

They did not seem to be any more spiritual than before.

Daniel could see no more than a few who were heartily seeking God, so he determined to do it himself. He behaved like a man with a cheque from heaven. The cheque promised return from exile, on condition of a renewed seeking of the Lord. As far as Daniel could see, nobody else was interested in cashing it. He therefore decided to do it alone, and set himself to seek God for the return of the exiled Jews.

Daniel did not say to himself, 'God has promised that it will happen, therefore whatever I do, or do not do, it will happen.' His logic was entirely different. It went like this: 'God has said that after seventy years we can go home. That is the divine promise. Therefore I will pray to Him to turn away His anger from Jerusalem, and to bring the promised return to pass.'

Too often in history people have made God's promises an excuse for doing nothing. Their approach has been fatalistic and they have sat in idleness, waiting for the promise to be fulfilled. Daniel knew nothing of such an approach. To him the divine promise was a *reason* to engage in the hard work of prayer, not an excuse for inactivity. He resolved to beseech his God to be favourable once more to Jerusalem. Within a few months Darius was gone, and Cyrus stood up to announce that the Jews could go home!

God had promised it. Daniel prayed for it. And it happened!

A great prayer

The prayer which Daniel prayed is one of the greatest in the Bible, and is preserved for us in verses 3 to 19. This is a long section, and we will not study every word and phrase of it. We will find more help if we extract from the prayer its main ingredients and seek to fix them in our memories.

Before we look at the six ingredients in the prayer, we should remind ourselves how important prayer is in the purposes of God. The cause of the Jews' return was His promise. But the cause of the return was also the prayer of the remnant.

Whatever other lessons we learn from this chapter, we must be sure to grasp this one. The cause of God's acting in history is not simply His promise, but also the prayer of His people. This is what praying 'according to His will' is all about. This is a

Daniel 9

subject on which the New Testament often speaks, and it is a frighteningly simple concept. Praying according to the will of God is finding out from the Scriptures what God has promised and praying for that.

Has God promised that the gospel will extend to the ends of the earth? He has. So let us pray for it — and it will happen!

Has God promised that when His Word goes out it will not return fruitlessly to Him? He has. So let us pray that His Word may have an effect on those who hear it — and it will!

Has God promised that His Son will come again, in glory and great power, and with all the holy angels? Yes, this is a clear and repeated promise in His Word. We therefore join with John to pray, 'Even so, come, Lord Jesus' (Revelation 22:20), and know that we will not be disappointed.

Daniel's approach was exactly the same. God had promised something, and this moved him to pray for it. And it happened!

In listing the ingredients of his prayer, the first that we notice is that he came to God *seriously*.

His habit had been to pray to the Lord three times a day. But for him this did not rule out periods of special prayer. In verse 3 we read that he set his face to seek the Lord God, 'to seek by prayer and supplications, with fasting, and sackcloth, and ashes'. He prayed with an intensity over and above that which was a normal part of his regular devotional life.

We next notice that he came to God *reverently*. His was not the sickening sort of 'sweet Jesus' prayer which is so popular today. He was intimate with God, but could nonetheless never forget that it was *God* with whom he was intimate. As he approached Him, he had a great sense of God's otherness — His Godhood. This is why his prayer begins, 'O Lord, the great and dreadful God ...' (4).

The third ingredient is that he prayed *penitently*. When we look at the beginning of the prayer, we read that it is a 'confession' (4), and the end of the prayer tells us the same thing (20). It is the prayer of a humble man seeking the great and dreadful God, and overcome with a sense of sin which he confesses. In this confession he cannot disaffiliate himself from the nation to which he belongs, and therefore the sins mentioned on his lips are the sins of the whole nation.

This does not mean that his confession was only a general thing. A study of the prayer reveals how very specific it was.

'We have sinned against thee (8) ... we have rebelled against him (9) ... neither have we obeyed the voice of the Lord our God, to walk in his laws, which he set before us by his servants the prophets. Yea, all Israel have transgressed thy law, even by departing, that they might not obey thy voice (10–11) ... we obeyed not (14) ... we have sinned, we have done wickedly' (15).

It is a prayer of confession. The princes, the rulers and all the people are guilty of the same offence. God has spoken, and they have not listened. God has commanded, and they have not obeyed. God has done great things for them, and they have not been grateful.

From such confession Daniel goes on to acknowledge that the nation's troubles and its exile are the fruit of its sin. He also freely acknowledges that God is acting righteously in punishing them. This is clear from verse 7, but also from verse 14: '... For the Lord our God is righteous in all his works which he doeth.'

In verses 11 to 14 Daniel admits that all that has happened is nothing other than what Moses had promised would happen if the nation turned its back on God. The present punishment is the fulfilment of a divine promise! Did this realization help his faith when he began to plead for the fulfilment of another divine promise — the promise to end the exile?

But Daniel did not only come seriously, reverently and patiently. In this great prayer we also see that he came to God *trusting in His mercy.*

There is a conquering sweetness about verse 4: 'O Lord, the great and dreadful God, keeping the covenant and *mercy* to them that love him ...' He knew of God's majesty. He also knew of His infinite tenderness.

The same note sounds in verses 9 and 18: 'To the Lord our God belong mercies and forgivenesses, though we have rebelled against him; ... we do not present our supplications before thee for our righteousnesses, but for thy great mercies.' Part of the greatness of Daniel's prayer lies in the fact that he realized that God had not forgotten how to be merciful. It was on that ground that he was bold enough to approach Him and to confidently lay before Him his requests.

This brings us to our next point. Daniel came to God *with specific requests.* He saw Jerusalem, the temple and the people ruined, and asked God to turn away His anger and fury from them all and to look upon them again with favour. In such requests he phrased his petitions pointedly: 'Let thine anger and thy fury be turned away from thy city Jerusalem, thy holy mountain (16) ... cause thy face to shine upon thy sanctuary that is desolate (17) ... open thine eyes, and behold our desolations, and the city which is called by thy name (18) ... hearken and do; defer not ...' (19).

The final ingredient that we should notice is that Daniel came to God *with strong arguments and with importunity*. Like Moses before him, he gave God convincing reasons why He should hear him, and repeated his requests and reasons with fervour and urgency. This is one of the secrets of those who prevail with God.

For example, in verse 15, he reminded God that He had done a great act in history when He brought the people out of Egyptian captivity. This act had brought great renown to God. It was if Daniel was implying, 'You have already done great things for Your people, so why not again? To bring them out of captivity is not a new thing for You.'

In verse 16 he reminds God that the Jerusalem which is desolate is '*thy* Jerusalem, *thy* holy mountain'. Should He not, then, do something for the city? The people who are being reproached are '*thy* people'. Can God stand by and do nothing, when it is His own people, the very people that He brought out of Egypt, who are being treated so contemptuously?

The argument strengthens in verse 17. The temple in Jerusalem had been the only place in the whole world devoted to the worship, and service of the true God. It was *that* building — 'thy sanctuary' — which now lay desolate. Will He not do something about it 'for the Lord's sake'?

The city in which that temple was situated, he reminds God, was also 'called by thy name' (18). Daniel's plea is not that God will act for Israel for the *people's* sake. They do not deserve it. They have forfeited all right to His favour on account of their rebellion and waywardness. But the fact still remains that they are known as God's people and named with His Name. Their continued desolation will reflect badly on God. It will appear as if He does not care for them, or that He is not powerful enough to help them. The world around will form its estimate of God on the basis of the welfare of the people who are known to be His people. God, then, *must* act, for His own sake. His own reputation and honour are at stake. If He does not step in to restore Israel, His Name will be dragged through the mud.

In this way Daniel marshals his arguments, and cries to God in an agony of spirit. The prayer reaches its crescendo in verse 19: 'O Lord, hear; O Lord, forgive; O Lord, hearken and do; defer not, for thine own sake, O my God: for thy city and thy people are called by thy name.'

When did *you* last pray like that? It is the sort of prayer that God hears.

If we would see God at work, we must find out what He has promised and pray for it like *that*. We do not need to wait until we are joined by others before we begin. It is when the *remnant* prays in this way that history is changed.

A great revelation

What happened as a result of this prayer? Verses 20 to 27 tell us. The great discovery had led to a great prayer. This was followed by a great revelation.

We do not know how long Daniel prayed, but he was still at it when evening came (21). It was while he was still overcome by the enormity of sin and its consequences and pleading for the future of God's cause, that the great revelation came.

His lips were still moving in prayer when Gabriel came again and touched him. He is immediately assured of a tremendous fact. He is told that from the very first moment that he began to pray heaven has been listening — and Gabriel's swift coming is the result! (23).

Was Daniel once more overcome with fear at the sight of his heavenly visitor? If so, he is immediately comforted. He is told that he is greatly loved in heaven, and has a reputation there! He is also told that he is to have a glimpse into the future of God's cause — the cause over which he has worried, and for which he has prayed (23). The angel has come to give him skill and understanding, so that he can grasp the revelation which is about to be made to him. 'Therefore,' he is told, 'understand the matter, and consider the vision.'

'Daniel,' said Gabriel (if I may paraphrase verses 24 and 25 a little!), 'You have been thinking about the figure of seventy years, and Israel and Jerusalem. Well, that is not the *only* seventy in God's programme for Jerusalem. In seventy weeks from now (or, as it is in Hebrew, in seventy 'sevens' or 'heptads',) Jerusalem will witness four things ...

'First of all Jerusalem will witness the finishing of transgressions, the end of sins and a reconciliation for iniquity. All that is one thing. The trangressions which stare God in the face will no longer do so. The sins which cry out for His punishment will be removed from His sight. Reconciliation will be made, to deal with the present iniquity which separates people from Him. Yes, seventy 'sevens' from now, something will be done about sin.'

What comfort these words must have brought to the elderly prophet! The enormity of sin had been a chief burden in his prayer. Now he is hearing that sin is to be dealt with!

'The second point is that in seventy "sevens" from now, everlasting righteousness will be brought in.'

The gospel, as we know, is not just about the pardon of sins. The wiping out of our record of guilt leaves us only neutral in the sight of God. The gospel promises more than that. It tells us how sinners may be commended to an offended God. It brings them to be righteous in His eyes.

'Thirdly, seventy "sevens" from now, visions and prophecy will be sealed up. Imagine the old scrolls. When you come to the end of one you roll it up and seal it. It means you have finished. Well, there have been a whole host of prophecies and visions looking forward to the future, and they will all be fulfilled seventy "sevens" from now.

'Finally, seventy "sevens" from now, the Most Holy will be anointed.'

Of course the word 'anointed' and the word 'Messiah' or 'Christ' are in essence the same word. The Messiah who comes will be the Most Holy God! All this Jerusalem will see. Seventy 'sevens' are determined, and this is what Gabriel announces they hold for the future.

On hearing all this Daniel must have been filled with immeasurable excitement. For the greater part of his life he had been grieving over Jerusalem and longing for its restoration. Now he was hearing that seventy 'sevens' from then it was going to have a future far exceeding all his expectations. The promised Christ would come, sin would be dealt with, and there would be a way by which sinners could be everlastingly right with God. The time of predicting Him would be over. He will have come — to Jerusalem!

He knew this because the angel told him. But that was not all that Gabriel had to say. In verses 25 to 27 he told Daniel how the seventy 'sevens' would be divided. There were to be three periods, two of which are mentioned in verse 25 and the third in verses 26 and 27.

The first period will be seven 'sevens' long. The second will be sixty-two 'sevens'. Then there will be one further 'seven' at the end. The division of the period is simple and easy to remember.

The starting-point for the period is 'the commandment to restore and to build Jerusalem', and from then until the Messiah will be the first two divisions of seven and sixty-two 'sevens' respectively (25). The ending of the first period of seven 'sevens' will be when 'the street shall be built again, and the wall, even in troublous times'. This must surely refer to the time of Ezra and Nehemiah.

Following this will be the second division of sixty-two 'sevens', during which nothing is predicted as happening. It is *after* the expiry of that second division of 'sevens' that the Messiah shall 'be cut off, but not for himself' (26).

In the light of many fanciful interpretations of this passage which are being circulated today, it is important to stress precisely what Gabriel revealed. Messiah was to be cut off, not during the sixty-ninth 'week', but *after* it. His cutting-off is to take place during the seventieth 'week'.

Many readers will not understand why I am emphasizing this. Suffice it to say that a large body of Christians believe that the seventieth 'week' mentioned in this chapter has been postponed to the end of the world. This is clearly impossible. Gabriel plainly declares that the Messiah is to be cut off during that week. If the seventieth week has been postponed, it can only mean that no Saviour has yet died for us. We are still in our sins.

The modern interpretation does not accord with the facts. Messiah was cut off at the end of sixty-nine 'weeks' as predicted, but 'not for himself'. 'For he was cut off out of the land of the living: for the trangression of my people was he stricken' (Isaiah 53:8).

The Hebrew of verse 26 can also be translated, 'Messiah shall be cut off, and shall have nothing.' If that is a correct translation it probably refers to Christ's disowning of Jerusalem, when He finally said to the Jews, 'Behold, *your* house is left unto *you* desolate' (Matthew 23:38).

The outcome of Messiah's being cut off is predicted in verse 26: 'And the people of the prince that shall come shall destroy the city and the sanctuary; and the end thereof shall be with a flood, and unto the end of the war desolations are determined.' This is an obvious prophecy that Jerusalem and its temple will be destroyed as foreign armies come in like a flood and wreak havoc and destruction.

Daniel is seeing this in the sixth century B.C., but it did not happen until A.D.70, when Titus and his Roman legions fulfilled this prophecy exactly. The destruction of Jerusalem did not immediately follow Calvary, but it was an event which was determined by the fact that the Jews rejected Christ. It did not happen in the seventieth 'week', but was determined in the seventieth 'week'. Our Lord made it clear, both in His Olivet discourse and as He walked to the cross, that His rejection by the Jews would mean the destruction of their city and temple (Matthew 23:34–24:38; Luke 23:27–31).

We might be helped at this point by thinking back to Adam. He was told that He would die on the very day that he ate the forbidden fruit. But he did not literally drop down dead. That day he died spiritually, and his physical death followed as a certain result. In the same way, Jerusalem's destruction was made certain by the Jewish rejection of their Messiah, but it was some little time before the certain event occurred. It did not take place in the seventieth 'week', but was most surely part and parcel of the events of that 'week'.

What else is prophesied here concerning that final 'week'? 'And he shall confirm the covenant with many for one week' (27). And He did, announcing, 'This is my blood of the new testament, which is shed for many for the remission of sins' (Matthew 26:28).

'And in the midst of the week he shall cause the sacrifice and the oblation to cease.' He did this, too, because He was sacrificed once for all (see Hebrews 7:27). The veil of the temple was rent in two, and the way into the Holiest was permanently opened by His never-to-be-repeated sacrifice. There was no further need for the Old Testament rituals and oblations. In fact, the destruction of Jerusalem made it impossible, eventually, for them to be continued.

For further light on these points, and on the remainder of verse 27, we can do no better than to quote E.B. Pusey. We are hesitant to quote an Anglo-Catholic, but we remember that Dr Pusey was an unrivalled scholar of the Old Testament prophets and had a rare insight in dealing with them. This is what he wrote last century concerning verses 26 and 27 of our chapter: 'All this meets in one in the Gospel. He, the so long looked-for, came: He *was* owned as the Messiah; he *did* cause the sacrifices of the law to cease; he *was* cut off; yet he *did* make the covenant with the many; a foreign army *did* desolate the city and Temple; the Temple for these 1800 years has lain desolate; the typical sacrifices have ceased, not through disbelief in their efficacy on the part of those to whom they were once given.'

The old book proved true

Daniel, then, was privileged to see that the present exile would cease. He was also privileged to see that the Christ would come — and to see what He would do, and where, and *when*.

We must be careful to note that the passage does not say that the 'weeks' are periods of seven years. The Hebrew simply speaks of seventy 'sevens' or 'heptads'. A great deal of the book of Daniel is symbolic, and we ought to be very careful before we give a literal interpretation to any of its numbers. This is especially true of the numbers seven and ten, which figure so prominently in biblical symbolism. We should think more than twice before we conclude that seventy 'sevens' equal four hundred and ninety years.

When Jeremiah used the number seventy, he was quite specific. He spoke of 'years'. Gabriel was more cryptic when he spoke of 'heptads'.

Having said that, it remains a matter of great interest that about eighty years or so after the events of this chapter, Artaxerxes I gave the command to rebuild Jerusalem. There was a 'going forth of the commandment to restore and to build Jerusalem' (25). Within forty-nine years (seven times seven) of that command, the city was rebuilt under the ministries of

Ezra, Nehemiah and others.

Four hundred and thirty-four years after that (sixty-two times seven) brings us to the late twenties of the first century A.D. It was at that time that, after three and a half years of ministry (half a 'week' or 'heptad'), our Lord Jesus Christ was cut off. Within three and a half more years, the apostles announced that the future lay, not with the Jews, upon whom judgement had fallen, but with the Gentiles.

These figures cannot be worked out exactly, and all attempts to do so have failed. No scholar anywhere, even those armed with calculators and computers, can make these figures perfectly fit his scheme.

But let us suppose that someone picked up Daniel chapter 9, knowing when the prophet lived, and took the seventy 'sevens' to be four hundred and ninety years. By the time he had come to what we call A.D. 1, such a person would have been saying to himself, 'The time is getting close. If I am right, the person of whom Daniel wrote is likely to be born any time now ...'

I have a theory — and it is *only* a theory. My theory is that because Daniel was so prominent in the early days of the Medo-Persian empire, his writings were placed in the libraries of Persia.

It *is* only a theory, but my theory is that even in the ancient world there were people who went into libraries and did research and attempted to get whatever the ancient form of a Ph.D. degree happened to be! They took down the ancient documents from the shelves, hoping to find something original or unusual to write about. My theory is that they took down Daniel's documents somewhere around 4 B.C., and said to themselves, 'The time is getting close. The Messiah spoken of in this chapter, if he is going to come at all, may perhaps be being born at this very moment.'

At that time these same scholars examined the heavens and saw a star which completely perplexed them, but which gave to them the indication that a great king had been born. They hurried back to Daniel's writings, and saw that the great king should be born about that time, and that he could be found in Jerusalem.

These wise men from the east then jumped on to their camels, carrying gold, frankincense and myrrh, went post-haste to Jerusalem, and enquired, 'Where is he that is born

King of the Jews?' (Matthew 2:2.)

All that is only theory. But what I *do* know is that in the city at that precise moment were humble souls filled with expectancy. Somehow they *knew* that the time of Messiah's coming was near. From their Old Testament Scriptures they knew very well that He would be born in Bethlehem, yet they were looking for redemption in *Jerusalem*! (Luke 2:38.)

How did they know all this? Is it feasible that they had concluded from the book of Daniel that the time was near, and that He would be recognized in the holy city, to which He was bound to come? Whichever way it was, it was revealed by the Holy Spirit to one of them, an old man, 'that he should not see death, before he had seen the Lord's Christ'.

'And he came by the Spirit into the temple: and when the parents brought in the child Jesus, to do for him after the custom of the law, then took he him up in his arms, and blessed God, and said, Lord, now lettest thou thy servant depart in peace, according to thy word: for mine eyes have seen thy salvation, which thou hast prepared before the face of all people; a light to lighten the Gentiles, and the glory of thy people Israel' (Luke 2:27–32).

And old lady also came in at that same moment and 'gave thanks likewise unto the Lord, and spake of him to all them that looked for redemption in Jerusalem' (Luke 2:38).

The old book proved true. The Christ came, just as it had been written of Him, and the old couple died happy.

The old book always proves true. It truly portrays Christ, and we can rest on what it says — not only with regard to time, but also with regard to eternity.

12.
AN OLD MAN SEES A VISION

Please read Daniel chapter 10

This wonderful chapter is full of powerful lessons for us, especially as far as our prayer life is concerned.

All the previous chapters of Daniel have been self-contained units. Each one has stood on its own. Chapter 10 is not like that at all. Its task is to introduce a vision, the details of which are found in chapters 11 and 12. It tells us of the circumstances in which the final vision of the book was given, but we must wait to read the two following chapters to see exactly what that vision was.

When and where the vision took place

The first four verses of the chapter tell us when and where the vision took place. It is now the third year of King Cyrus (1). Over two years have gone by since this Persian emperor had decreed that the Jews could return to Jerusalem to rebuild both the city and its temple. Zerubbabel and a small group of others had already set off and had arrived safely in Palestine. But Daniel had not joined them. There was still work for him to do in Persia. Besides, he was now eighty-six or eighty-seven, and it was a bit late in life to be travelling long distances and engaging in heavy building work.

The old man had prayed for the exiles to return, but had not gone himself. This did not mean that God had finished with him. He is going to give a further revelation to His elderly prophet. The frail servant of God is going to see things that he has not seen in any of his previous visions. He is going to see the Son of God again and also have a further insight into the future. And what is about to be unveiled to him is going to be clear (1).

Daniel is now old, but not too old for special religious exercises (2–3). For three whole weeks he has been mourning and has been cast down. He has cut out all pleasant food and delicacies. He has stopped eating meat. He has put aside his wine. He is no longer using the anointing oil, which is widely used in the East to refresh oneself. He has given himself to sincere and deep humiliation. It is a time of sorrow and fasting.

What is the reason for all this? Why should this old man set aside three weeks for sorrowful fasting and prayer?

We are not specifically told, but we can work it out from what we know of Old Testament history. Daniel had longed and prayed that the Jews should be permitted to return from exile, and his prayer had been answered in the decree of Cyrus. A few Jews had already returned. Yet it was almost as if no return had taken place at all. Only a small minority had availed itself of the God-given opportunity to go back. The vast majority had no real desire to go home.

This must have been heartbreaking for Daniel. For seventy years and more, Jerusalem had never been out of his thoughts. He had prayed three times a day with his windows open towards the city he loved and had never forgotten. It was a love which his fellow-countrymen evidently did not share. They were happier where they were and showed such little interest in returning from exile. Who knew how long the official permission to do so might last? Perhaps the door of return would soon be shut tightly again.

Not only so, but the few who had returned were facing unprecedented difficulties in their task of rebuilding the city and the temple. The foundations of the temple had been successfully laid, but the work had now stopped because of opposition from the Samaritans, who had appealed to Persia for their own opinion of the work to be considered. The returned exiles were unspeakably discouraged.

Daniel had prayed for the return, but it had turned out to be a very poor thing. It looked as if the few who had gone back had done so for nothing. It appeared as if it was all in vain. The situation hardly looked like a fulfilment of what God had promised through Jeremiah.

This was why Daniel was cast down, and why he was praying. It was at this point that God, in His tender mercy, gave him the final vision of the book, which we are about to

Daniel 10 131

study.

Daniel tells us in verse 4 of the exact date on which it took place. It was three days after the conclusion of the feast of the Passover and Unleavened Bread. The newly returned exiles celebrated this in the promised land, for the first time in three generations. While they did so, the ageing Daniel was beside the River Tigris. It was at that time and place that he received this final vision.

What he saw and heard, and how he reacted

Verses 5 to 9 tell us what Daniel saw and heard. They also tell us how he reacted.

By the River Tigris he lifted up his eyes and saw a man clothed in linen. Consistently throughout the Bible this description refers to a heavenly visitor. Around the visitor's waist was a girdle of the very finest gold. The picture is one of dazzling splendour and majesty.

The description of the visitor continues in verse 6. We should compare what we read there with what John wrote in Revelation 1:13-17, where he saw 'One like unto the Son of man, clothed with a garment down to the foot, and girt about the paps with a golden girdle. His head and his hairs were white like wool, as white as snow; and his eyes were as a flame of fire; and his feet like unto fine brass, as if they burned in a furnace; and his voice as the sound of many waters. And he had in his right hand seven stars: and out of his mouth went a sharp twoedged sword: and his countenance was as the sun shineth in his strength. And when I saw him, I fell at his feet as dead. And he laid his right hand upon me, saying unto me, Fear not; I am the first and the last ...'

When John wrote that, he was exiled on the Isle of Patmos, and was describing the prophetic vision of the Lord Jesus Christ that he had there. There is considerable overlap between what John saw and what Daniel saw. There can be no doubt that the mourning Daniel saw none other than the Son of God! Many times in Old Testament days, long before He actually assumed human flesh in Mary's womb, the Lord Jesus Christ appeared in the form of a man. Such a phenomenon is called a 'theophany', and the one in this chapter is not the first in the book of Daniel, as we have seen. Once more, Daniel saw the pre-incarnate Lord of glory!

It is plain from verse 7 that the glorious vision was seen by Daniel alone. It was unveiled only to the spiritually perceptive. Only a man with a spiritual nature is able to look into the spiritual world.

Daniel's experience at this point bears some similarity to that of Paul on the Damascus Road. When the Lord Jesus Christ addressed Paul, everybody heard the sound of His voice, but only Paul heard the words which were spoken (Acts 9:7; 22:9). In the same way, only Daniel saw the vision. Everybody else felt the presence of the heavenly Visitor, but they saw nothing. The nearness of the Son of God caused them to tremble and, intimidated by the holy presence, they ran and hid themselves. There was an overwhelming sense of heaven on earth. Once the others had fled, Daniel was left alone with the Son of God.

'Therefore I was left alone, and saw this great vision, and there remained no strength in me: for my comeliness was turned in me into corruption, and I retained no strength' (8).

An old and faithful believer is now alone with the second Person of the blessed Trinity! The strength goes out of his mortal body and his natural colour turns into a deathly pallor. The voice whose words are 'like the voice of a multitude' speaks to him.

Such an experience is too much for the mortal human frame to bear. Daniel falls in prostration, his face to the ground, and passes out. The old prophet loses consciousness at the feet of the Lord Jesus Christ!

Sometimes we hear men and women speak defiantly of our Lord. They say that when the judgement comes, they will 'tell Him a thing or two'. But it will not be like that at all. When men and women see the Lord Jesus Christ in His unveiled splendour, the strength ebbs out of them and they fall at His feet. Who can describe the majesty of the Son of God? To mortal people He is a terrifying and overcoming sight.

What the Visitor said

What our Lord Jesus Christ now said to Daniel is recorded in

Daniel 10 133

verses 10 to 14.

First of all, however, the elderly prophet had to be restored to consciousness. This did not take place all at once, and the beginning of the process is described in verse 10. A hand shook and roused Daniel. This awoke him sufficiently for him to be able to come up into a kneeing position, with his palms on the ground. But some more words of comfort will be necessary before He can stand upright.

These are given to him in verse 11. The gracious Saviour speaks to him by name, and comfortably assures him that he is a man greatly loved. One can hardly think of anything more marvellous which a sinner might want to hear. The Son of God loved him!

He is told to give careful attention to the words which the Visitor has been sent to speak to him, and to stand on his feet as he does so. This he does, but not without continuing to tremble. He is in very great trepidation because of what he is about to hear from the lips of the Son of God. He is far more overcome than he was on the previous occasion, when he met Gabriel. This is because the glory of God is infinitely greater than that of the most glorious of angels. He fell like a dead man at Gabriel's feet, but recovered quite quickly. In this chapter he hardly recovers at all, and as we see here and later, all his recovery was because of the imparting of supernatural strength. The glory of God is too much for the unaided human frame to endure.

In his terror he hears the Saviour address him again by name. He tenderly consoles him with the assurance that there is no need to be afraid. The Visitor is a Friend (12).

'Three weeks ago, Daniel, you began to pray, and from the first moment that you did so you were heard. You set yourself to understand the future of God's people and you began to chasten yourself because of their sins. The moment that you began you were heard, and I was sent. That is the reason that you are now going to receive the revelation that I bring you. For three whole weeks you have been praying, but I have been hindered in coming...'

Verse 13 is certainly one of the most mysterious verses in the Old Testament. Who could possibly have hindered the Lord Jesus Christ? The answer given is 'the prince of the kingdom of Persia'.

We should notice the exact words which are used. It was the 'prince' and *not* the 'king' of Persia. It was not Darius or Cyrus who had withstood Christ. In the Bible they are consistently referred to as 'kings'. That is the title given to such earthly potentates. The verse is not about them, but about 'the *prince* of the kingdom of Persia'.

To understand this we must remember some teaching given by the apostle Paul in 1 Corinthians 10:20. He tells us there that when people worship idols, it is not the idols that they worship at all despite what the worshippers may themselves think. Behind idol worship are demons and these are the actual gods of idol-worshippers.

In the same way, behind the national gods of Persia were supernatural and evil personalities. It was these evil spirits who had moved the Persian authorities to support the Samaritans against the small group of faithful Jews who had returned to Palestine from exile. The situation had continued for some time but, twenty-one days earlier, Daniel had summoned heavenly aid. Christ had come into the situation, and the archangel Michael with Him. Spiritual battle had been joined.

The outcome of the spiritual battle is reflected in the end of verse 13. This no longer refers to the 'prince of the kingdom of Persia' but to 'the kings of Persia' — that is, the earthly rulers of that empire. The evil spirits who previously moved them to do evil are no longer next to them. Instead Christ and Michael are there. The forces of God have triumphed and it is they who now move and influence the Persian kings in their decision-making. The situation relating to the returned exiles is going to be changed.

Not only has the situation changed, but Christ has come to reveal to Daniel what the future holds. He is to have a long glimpse into the future, and is to see what will befall the people of God (14). The vision will extend not only to the immediate years ahead, but to the end of the world. The revelation is going to be detailed. Chapters 11 and 12 of Daniel are two of the most remarkable chapters in the Bible. They record history which was written in considerable detail *before the event.* It was to unveil all that they record that Christ came to Daniel by the Tigris that day.

Daniel 10 135

How Daniel was made capable of receiving the vision to follow

We have discovered when and where the vision took place. We have seen how Daniel saw and heard Christ and how he reacted. We have studied our Lord's opening words to him. The remainder of the chapter, from verse 15, tells us how the prophet was made capable of receiving the vision which is to occupy the next two chapters.

The fact is that, despite the comforting words that he has heard, and even despite the divine command, the 'Fear not', Daniel has still not yet regained his composure. Once more he falls prostrate at the feet of Christ, overcome with reverence and awe (15). His meeting with the Lord is so overwhelming that he is rendered speechless. He is literally dumbfounded. He is too astonished by it all to bring so much as a word to his mouth.

So it is that one in human form — an angel, of course — touches him, much as one of the seraphim touched Isaiah when *he* saw Christ (Isaiah 6:5-6). By means of the supernatural strength thus imparted, the prophet regains his power of speech. He is able to stumble out a few words explaining how he has been overcome with anguish, and how he has lost all his strength (16). He asks how he, a mere servant, can talk with his Lord (17). He explains how the vision of holiness is too much for him, and how the physical effect of it has left him at death's door.

The response to this is that once more an angel appears and supernaturally strengthens the prophet (18). He is recovering by degrees, but is still not in a state of readiness to hear the revelation which is to be given. The remaining strength that he needs becomes his when once more the Son of God speaks to him in affectionate and endearing terms. The tender voice twice commands him to 'be strong', and at last the frail old believer is able to reply, 'Let my lord speak; for thou hast strengthened me' (19). The mortal man is ready for the supernatural vision. He has been given sufficient strength to receive the amazing revelations which are now to be given to him.

'There is a spiritual conflict with Persia going on,' says the Lord in verses 20 and 21, if we may paraphrase Him, 'and I am going to return to it. When that is over, there will be a spiritual conflict with the prince of Greece. In these struggles I have no ally except Michael, your prince ...'

'But do you know why I am here? Do you know why I have come to you? It is to show you what is written in God's plan for the future.'

The Authorized Version speaks of these plans as 'the scripture of truth'. They were not yet written down as Scripture, but were already written down in the plan of the Lord. The purpose of the expression is to emphasize the absolute certainty of the detailed events to be predicted in the vision which occupies the next two chapters.

Some lessons for us to learn

Before we pass on to examine that vision, we should not overlook the weighty lessons which Daniel 10 has to teach us.

This chapter shows us who are the real enemies of the work of God. This point is of considerable importance, and we must not leave the chapter without making due note of it.

Zerubbabel had gone back to Jerusalem. The whole work which he and his few companions hoped to undertake had been held up. Who is to be held responsible?

Should we blame the discouraged band itself? Are we to say to them, 'It is all your fault. It is your discouragement which is holding things up. Discouraged people are the real enemies of the work of God'?

Or should we blame the Samaritans? They had been living in Palestine throughout the whole time of the Jewish exile in Babylon. They were more than upset by the return of the Jews and their plan to rebuild the temple. It was the last thing they wanted, and they therefore set about trying to stop it. Should we then say that the real enemies of God's work are its critics and physical opponents?

Or is it the Persians who should carry the blame? It was the Persian authorities who first gave permission for the Jews to return and then ordered the work to stop when the Samaritans complained. Surely they are the real rogues.

None of these are the real enemies of the work of God. The real enemies are revealed in verses 13 and 20: 'The prince of the kingdom of Persia withstood me.' 'I will return to fight with the prince of Persia.'

It is no longer popular to state this, but it nonetheless remains true that the Bible contains a definite doctrine of angels. There are good angels, and there are also evil ones, who are also known as 'demons'.

It is the clear teaching of the Word of God that evil men on earth are directed by evil powers. It is these evil spiritual personalities, which influence and penetrate human minds, that are the real enemies of God's work.

The warfare in which we are engaged is not primarily a warfare with our own discouragement or with visible enemies. It is not primarily a warfare with critics, or with authorities who constantly frustrate the things that we want to do. Our warfare is a spiritual warfare with spiritual enemies. This is clear from the chapter we have just studied, and is a fact underlined by the apostle Paul when he wrote, 'For we wrestle not against flesh and blood, but against principalities, against powers, against the rulers of the darkness of this world, against spiritual wickedness (or wicked spirits) in high places' (Ephesians 6:12).

There is a realm of the spiritual. There is an invisible conflict which is made visible in our own experiences. It is very important that we recognize this. For example, often when we speak to others of the gospel, their reply is 'I don't understand.' When this happens our natural reaction is to be discouraged and to blame their lack of understanding, or their lack of intellectual ability.

This is not the problem. Nor should we blame our lack of success on bad communication — although there is plenty of that around. Nor should we conclude that it is our methods which are at fault — though these, too, should be constantly under review. Nor is the essential problem the unhappy fact that we often do the Lord's work in the wrong spirit.

The reason why men and women do not believe the gospel when it is explained to them is because 'the god of this world hath blinded the minds of them which believe not, lest the light of the glorious gospel of Christ, who is the image of God, should shine unto them' (2 Corinthians 4:4). The devil and his cohorts are the real enemies of the work of God.

Once we understand this, we also grasp the importance of a

second lesson which the chapter teaches us. *It shows us what are the only weapons appropriate for the conflict in which we are engaged.*

Paul moves immediately from identifying our true enemies to the command: 'Take unto you the whole armour of God, that ye may be able to withstand in the evil day, and having done all, to stand' (Ephesians 6:13).

The armour we don and the weapons we wield are decided by the kind of conflict in which we are engaged. Because our warfare is spiritual it is imperative that we resort to spiritual protection and weaponry. If we do not, it will soon be all up with us.

Consequently, the apostle enumerates the pieces of armour which are required for the battle, but closes by mentioning a weapon for which there is no earthly picture: 'Praying always with all prayer and supplication in the Spirit, and watching thereunto with all perseverance and supplication for all saints; and for me, that utterance may be given unto me, that I may open my mouth boldly, to make know the mystery of the gospel' (Ephesians 6:18-19).

The spiritual conflict requires that we resort to prayer. By what other means can heavenly aid be summoned? Daniel 10:12 encourages us to realize that from the moment we begin to pray, help is on the way. Like Daniel we may have to agonize for a long time — perhaps for three weeks — before we receive any personal assurance that our prayer has been heard. But we are heard from the moment we open our mouths.

There is tremendous power in prayer. It was by prayer that the exile was ended and that Cyrus was moved to make his historic decree. When the work of rebuilding was held up, it was to prayer that Daniel resorted again. It was not long afterwards that the work recommenced. The enemies were frustrated and God sent new leaders to exhort and encourage the people. At last the temple was rebuilt, and nothing proved able to prevent it.

Think of it! An old man of eighty-seven, in a distant country, prayed — and history was changed!

This is why we should be eager to pray for the cause of Christ both locally and beyond. The power of prayer is beyond calculation. This is another point which was constantly emphasized by the apostle Paul. His letters are full of requests

Daniel 10

for prayer. He knew that when God's people gave themselves to prayer, things were certain to change. His appeals to strive together in this exercise are constant. He does not expect his readers to hold back until they realize precisely how prayer wields this immense power. It is enough to know that the moment we pray is the moment when we import heavenly aid in to the spiritual conflict. Christ and the armies of Michael join battle with the forces of evil, and the situation is inevitably changed.

At this point there is a third lesson to learn from the chapter. *It shows us what the praying person may expect.*

At no time in his long life did Daniel exercise greater power than he did here. But never was he more weak and humbled. Never was he more broken down and prostrated.

It is true that prayer summons divine power and heavenly aid. But it never exalts the man who prays. It abases him.

The way of prayer is solitary and difficult. When the answer does not come at once, it is also perplexing. But there are great consolations in it.

In the place of prayer Daniel saw the Son of God in His unveiled majesty, and heard from His lips that he was greatly loved in heaven. He was touched by angels. He was assured that the present situation would be changed. He saw that all is ultimately well in the future, because God rules it. Where could he have seen any of these things, other than in the place of prayer?

Where else, but in the place of prayer, can a weak, trembling, mortal sinner experience *heaven on earth*?

13.
HISTORY IS HIS STORY

Please read Daniel 11:1-20

This chapter of Daniel follows directly on from the last. As it opens, the Lord Jesus Christ is still speaking. The first verse belongs properly to the previous chapter, and it is hard to see why those who made the chapter divisions did so at this point.

In the opening verse the Lord is saying that when the Persian Empire took over, it was *He* who strengthened Michael at that stage of the heavenly conflict. Babylon was overthrown by the power of Christ. The Medes and Persians were His earthly instruments, but the actual overthrow of that earthly empire was a divine act brought about by the Son of God Himself.

The remainder of the chapter is summed up in the opening words of verse 2: 'And now will I show thee the truth ...' The Lord is going to give Daniel a true picture of the future. Chapter 11 consists of history which was written *before* it took place! It had been written eternally in the divine books (10:21), but was even to be written in *Daniel's* book a considerable time before it happened.

Chapter 11 is one of the most difficult chapters of Daniel and, as we study it, we shall need to refer constantly to the Bible open before us. The chapter is hard work, especially for those who are not good at history. This is why, for the purpose of study, we are splitting it up. But it has powerful and heartening lessons to teach us. When we see them, we will consider that all our effort has been more than worthwhile.

We will first of all look at the contents of 11:1-20. Even if we master these in only the most general way, we shall be in a position to learn the lessons which will so greatly strengthen our spiritual lives.

Daniel 11:1-20 141

The contents

2. As our Lord speaks to Daniel in this vision, it is the third year of the reign of Cyrus of Persia (10:1). He tells Daniel that the fourth king after the present one 'shall be far richer than they all: and by his strength through his riches he shall stir up all against the realm of Grecia.' He will be somebody special.

The fourth king of Persia after Cyrus was the renowned Xerxes. Richer than any of his predecessors, he used his considerable wealth to raise and maintain an immense army, by which he went and attacked Greece. I still have vivid memories of how my boyish heart thrilled at the reading of *The History of Herodotus*, which records these exploits and gives accounts of the famous battles at Thermopylae and Salamis. History was fulfilled exactly as the Lord had predicted to the elderly prophet.

3-4. But Persia did not remain the dominant power. Before long the glory of the world was Greece, which was led into prominence by Alexander the Great, to whom verse 3 refers. This exceptional young man died in Babylon in the prime of his life, at the young age of thirty-two. None of his sons inherited the empire and twelve of his generals divided the spoils among themselves. It was a time of plotting and counter-plotting, and eventually the empire settled down to being divided into four distinct sections — something previously prophesied in Daniel 8:8. A few other petty kingdoms survived for a while, but the final outcome was that the glory of Alexander's empire faded away and became four kingdoms, none of which knew anything of the power or glory of the original empire.

In this way the predictions of verse 4 were exactly fulfilled, as a close examination of it will bear out. Our method in this chapter should now be plain. We are telling the history of the inter-testamental period, while referring to the specific verses which predicted these events as we go along.

5. The next thing to be predicted concerns the king of 'the south'. This term undoubtedly refers to Egypt, as verse 8 makes plain. 322 B.C. witnessed the rise of a certain Ptolemy Soter, who came to rule Egypt that year and did so until 305 B.C. He took under his wing a prince by the name of Seleucus, who turned out to be militarily brilliant and was soon one of his generals. In 312 B.C. this young man took Babylon from all

rivals and set up what became a separate Seleucid empire in the north, based on Syria. Very soon it greatly exceeded the southern kingdom of the Ptolemies, both in size and power.
6. After some time these two kingdoms of the south and the north formed an alliance through a marriage. This, in fact, took place thirty-five years after the death of Seleucus. Berenice, daughter of Ptolemy Philadelphus of the south, was taken with great pomp to be the wife of Antiochus II in the north. But the marriage did not have the desired effect of bringing the two kingdoms together. Shortly afterwards, Berenice's father died. The story is too long to tell in such a book as this, but suffice it to say that very soon she herself was dead; so was her husband Antiochus II, and so was their child. All of them were murdered. Before very long it was as if there had never been a Queen Berenice, or any support for a north-south *rapprochement*.
7. 'A branch of her roots' — in fact, her brother — became the next king of Egypt. He was the third Ptolemy to rule there, and became known as Ptolemy Euergetes ('the Well-doer'). He had a pitched battle with the north, and succeeded in putting to death those who had murdered his sister.
8. The success of his southern kingdom was vast. His armies spoiled the north, and carried its protective gods back with them to Egypt. For a while there was a considerable superiority of the Ptolemies over the Seleucids.
  The Authorized Version reads at the end of verse 8: '... and he shall continue more years than the king of the north.' This can alternatively be translated, 'He shall refrain for some years from attacking the king of the north.' And he did. All these historical details were revealed to Daniel centuries before they occurred. As the chapter proceeds, surely we are beginning to be amazed at the predictive accuracy of the Word of God!
9. There is no possibility that the Authorized Version is correct in its translation of verse 9. It should undoubtedly be translated, 'And he (the king of the north) will enter the realm of the king of the south, and will return to his land.'
  This is what happened. Out of the north came a man with the lovely name of Seleucus Callinicius. In 240 B.C. he marched against Ptolemy in the south and thoroughly defeated him. He then returned to his own land.
10. After that the two sons of the northern king, Seleucus

Daniel 11:1-20

Ceraunus and Antiochus the Great, stirred themselves for battle. The language of verse 10 is most careful and specifically predicts what happened next. The alliance of the two princes was broken, as Seleucus perished on the battlefield, and Antiochus the Great had to continue alone. He conducted a number of expeditions in many different directions, until he took Gaza on the very edge of the Ptolemaic kingdom. This brought north and south into open conflict once more.

11. Antiochus' militia was immense. In comparison the southern kingdom had almost nothing — 70,000 infantry, 5,000 cavalry and 73 elephants! However, motivated by the fury of Ptolemy Philopator, the southern forces engaged the vastly superior forces of the north — and won! The northern multitude was 'given into his hand'.

12. The surprise and wonder of this unexpected victory filled the southern king with pride, and he began to inflict even greater defeats on the north. But he did not gain any lasting advantages from this and went south again to an easy life.

13. The southern superiority was not to last. Not long afterwards Ptolemy Philopator died, to be succeeded by a child of four! Once more the north was the dominant power in the area.

14. It now looked as if everything was up for the south. Philip of Macedon joined in league with the north, and thus considerably strengthened the south's enemies. Rebels appeared within Egyptian borders, though they did not last long. All these historical details occurred 'to establish the vision'. In other words, as each historical event fulfilled what had been so specifically predicted by our Lord to Daniel, the vision was increasingly confirmed as being truthful. All that had been predicted was coming true in front of the readers' eyes! There was nothing false in it. It was obvious that the book could be trusted entirely. This was to prove a tremendous encouragement when the Lord's people went through dark times and learned from the same pages what the ultimate outcome was to be!

15. The north then had a decisive victory at Sidon. The city was beseiged and earthworks were used to enable the attacking army to get into the town.

16. It seemed as if Antiochus the Great had become invincible. Nobody was able to withstand him, and he therefore did exactly as he wanted. Palestine was quickly in his hands, and began to suffer seriously as a result.

17. But despite all his efforts he still could not defeat the south. It was at this point that he changed his tactics and we come to a period of history which some have wrongly confused with that in Shakespeare's play *Antony and Cleopatra.*

Antiochus concluded that the best way to defeat the south was by subtlety. Very plausibly he went to Egypt with all sorts of upright friends and betrothed his daughter, Cleopatra, to the Ptolemaic king. He thought that the outcome of the arrangement would be that he would at last be able to assert his power over the south, which he had failed to defeat for so long.

The plan failed miserably. After the marriage, five years later, Cleopatra did not live up to her father's expectations and constantly sided with her husband against him. The divine prediction was once more exactly correct: 'But she shall not stand on his side, neither be for him.'

18. This led Antiochus the Great to abandon his ambitions towards the south and to turn them towards 'the isles' — that is, the coastlands of the Mediterranean Sea. It was particularly in his mind to annexe Asia Minor to his dominions. This time he had bitten off more than he could chew. Towards him marched the Roman, Lucius Scipio Asiaticus. Antiochus was utterly defeated and humiliated.

19. It was an enormous defeat and the end of Antiochus' territorial ambitions. No longer able to attack foreign lands, he concentrated his attention on home affairs, where he soon disappeared off the scene.

20. He was replaced by Seleucus Philopator. One of his early acts was to send an emissary called Heliodorus to seize the funds of the temple treasury at Jerusalem. Heliodorus set off to do it, but reported that an apparition had warned him about doing such a wicked act. It was certainly never done. Seleucus Philopator mysteriously disappeared very soon afterwards — within just a few weeks of beginning his reign. It is generally believed that Heliodorus poisoned him. It was a striking fulfilment of the prediction: 'But within few days he shall be destroyed, neither in anger, nor in battle.'

All this history is difficult and complicated, and not particularly interesting. It is almost impossible for anyone to remember for long the precise history of the relationships

Daniel 11:1-20

between the Ptolemies and the Seleucids. But we have come to the point where a certain Antiochus Epiphanes will come onto the stage of history. We have already read of him in Daniel 8. He is extremely important, and we shall learn a good deal about him in the next section of this book, which covers 11:21-45.

We should not be too concerned if we do not have a detailed grasp of Middle-Eastern history between the Old and New Testaments. Our survey of it in this chapter has been little more than superficial. Our aim has been simply to note that each detail predicted is exactly what happened. What was written in God's book, and then in Daniel's book, is precisely what is written in *our* history books. This astonishing fact should lead us to learn a number of very helpful spiritual lessons. They are as clear as crystal, and we come to them now.

Some lessons

First of all, *a chapter like this should renew and fortify our confidence in the Bible.*

As I have explained elsewhere, my purpose in writing this book has been to encourage people to read the book of Daniel for themselves. It is not part of my purpose to summon evidence in favour of my certain conviction that Daniel was written in the sixth century B.C. The book is a unit, and there is no evidence that any part of it was written at any other time. There is abundant internal and external evidence of its sixth-century date. This evidence can be found in the books by Professors Robert Dick Wilson and E.J. Young which are referred to on page 171. Those with the necessary mental equipment would profit unspeakably from a detailed study of those volumes. It needs to be noted that their arguments have often been ignored, but they have never been answered. This is, frankly, because they are unassailable.

What we have open before us is a fantastic piece of literature in which history was written before it took place! There can be no other explanation for such a phenomenon other than that it has a supernatural origin. No wonder that our Lord Jesus Christ could say of the Old Testament at large, and therefore of Daniel, 'Thy word is truth'! (John 17:17.)

The Bible is not just a book with truths in it; it is not just a true book; it is a book which *is* truth. The vast majority of men and women around us simply do not know what to believe, or where to turn. They are crying out for some sure word. They want something which they know for certain is the truth. We are able to tell them confidently to trust the Bible. God's Word is truth. It is infallible. It is inerrant.

Think of someone whom you know who always tells you the truth. You are sure this is so, because on every occasion his words have been capable of being verified they have been found to be truthful. Do you not believe such a person when he talks to you about things that you can *not* check up on?

It is the same with Scripture. In every area where it can be checked up on, it displays that it is telling us the truth. The verses of this chapter that we have studied are such an area. We are able to see what was predicted and can clearly see that the events of subsequent history exactly tallied with the predictions made. At every point it proved true.

This being so, why should I disbelieve the Bible when it speaks to me in other areas? It speaks to me with equal certainty about God. It tells me what to believe concerning Him, and the duty He requires from me. It also tells me about man — where he came from, why he is here and what is the real nature of his problem. In the same way it speaks about such weighty subjects as how to gain eternal life, how to live my personal life, what my family life should be like, my responsibilities as a citizen and a vast number of other important subjects. It is momentously reassuring to know that the book which speaks on all these subjects is entirely trustworthy. All I need to know for this life is contained in a book of 'true truth' — to use the expression of Dr Francis Schaeffer.

What folly it would be to ignore or neglect such a book! It would be an even greater folly to disbelieve or to doubt it! There is in this world a true book — true because it comes from God.

It is time for us to stop apologizing for the Bible. It is time to stop being timid about being evangelical when we are mixing with those who doubt and dispute the Scriptures and openly scorn those who love and trust them. We believe the Bible to be what it claims to be — the Word of God. This conviction is

Daniel 11:1-20 147

renewed and fortified when we read such an astonishing chapter as Daniel 11. An assurance is borne in upon our hearts by the Holy Spirit that we have open *a book of truth*!

Our second lesson from chapter 11 can be summarized in the old cliché: *'History is His story.'*

How could the Lord have given to Daniel a detailed survey of the future, if that future was out of His control?

Imagine what those who had this chapter in their hands must have thought when they saw the different Ptolemies and Seleucids coming and going in just the way that had been predicted. They would have said, 'Everything is coming to pass just as God said.' It would have been their sure conviction that He was in control and that His purposes were being carried out. What had been predicted had happened. They would have concluded that the things predicted which had not *yet* happened were *equally certain* to occur.

Whatever happens in history does so because it is written in God's book. In this case a particular period of history was revealed to Daniel and written in *his* book, too. Even if it had not been, it would not have altered the fact that it was written in the book of God. History is not without meaning or purpose, as some modern historians have declared. All that happens is bringing to pass the decrees of God. And yet He is in no sense the author of sin. He does not condone it for a moment. We do not understand how this can be so, but it remains a fact. We shall see all these things more clearly when we stand on a better shore and are able to look back on the history of the world.

There is immense comfort in this truth. As we survey today's world we see evil forces at work everywhere — lurking, threatening, persecuting and oppressing. But these, even these, are bringing to pass the eternal purposes of God. These forces are doing nothing different from the great world empires mentioned in the book of Daniel. We have learned that they were in the hands of God. That is no less true of forces today. History is not out of control and its outcome is not a matter of doubt. All things are moving towards the final triumph of our Lord Jesus Christ and the final and everlasting punishment of the wicked.

There is a third and final lesson for us to learn from this

passage. *God is still God – even when He is nowhere to be seen.*

We have seen the Lord Jesus Christ announce the future to the prophet Daniel. Yet when we examine the historical survey which He gave him, we find that there is not a single mention of God in it. There is a veritable catalogue of wars, alliances, marriages, battles and a confusing amount of coming and going. Man takes up all the picture. The strongest man of the hour constantly appears to be the one who is calling the tune. There is not a mention of God anywhere. To all appearances it seems as if history is nothing to do with Him.

And yet it is the Lord Himself who is announcing it all! This serves only to stress the lesson we have just learned. History is *His* story. This remains true, whether there is any sign of God being at work, or not.

Think of the historical period mentioned in this section. Armies were crossing and counter-crossing Palestine. The attention of the world was either on the Seleucids or the Ptolemies, and the Jews were simply not a fact at all in world politics.

Empires came and went, but the Jews counted for nothing. They were the only people in the world who had the truth about the living God, and yet they were entirely overlooked. To the world they were of no measurable significance. They had plenty of trouble, perplexity and persecution. Often their hearts were filled with fear. As far as the history books were concerned, their God was nowhere to be seen.

But even *then* events were proceeding exactly as the Saviour had predicted and His purposes, both for them in particular and for the world at large, were being fulfilled. Nothing was happening anywhere except that which had been previously written in His book. That remained true even when He seemed to be completely absent from His world. All history is His story. When He cannot be seen, He is there directing the world's affairs all the same.

As we close this chapter may I ask if you believe that? Really?

We live in days of apostasy, when men stand up in the name of Christ and proclaim nothing more than a form of religiously flavoured humanism. They take upon themselves the name of Christian, but are not mastered by any truly spiritual convictions, nor characterized by a reverence for, and a submission to the Word of God. Every day the visible church

Daniel 11:1-20 149

moves even further away from its apostolic foundations.

As a direct result of such manifold unfaithfulness there has been, and there continues, a moral landslide at every level in our society. In addition, we live under the shadow of nuclear terror; we witness daily shifts in international and national politics; and we read of universal economic confusion. We face the ever-increasing likelihood of being mugged in our own streets and robbed at our own firesides. We look around for some stemming of the evil tide, but we look in vain. There is hardly a prominent voice for the truth anywhere. We become increasingly reconciled to the unhappy fact that all hell could be let loose at any moment.

Even in *this* situation, can you believe what this chapter makes so evidently clear — that God is *still* God, even when He is nowhere to be seen?

> Thrice blest is he to whom is given
> The instinct that can tell
> That God is on the field when He
> Is most invisible.
>
> He hides Himself so wondrously,
> As though there were no God;
> He is least seen when all the powers
> Of ill are most abroad.

14.
Antiochus Epiphanes!

Please read Daniel 11:21–45

Daniel 11:25–45 is rather difficult terrain. First of all we shall set out to survey the ground, and then we shall extract from it some jewels.

It is a continuation of the vision which our Lord gave to the elderly prophet in the late sixth century B.C. Supernaturally strengthened by angels, the old man has been capable of receiving a vision of the future. He has been told that the Medo-Persian Empire will give way to Greece, which, after splitting into four, will later be dominated by the affairs of two kingdoms in particular. Up to verse 20 the chapter has given a detailed summary of the relationship between the southern kingdom of the Ptolemies, based on Egypt, and the northern kingdom of the Seleucids, based on Syria.

Our study of the vision has already fortified and strengthened our confidence in the Bible, and the section now before us will do the same. Our method of study will be similar to our last chapter. Without being side-tracked by too many historical details, we will spell out the history of the period in the plainest way possible. As we do so, we will refer to the individual verses of the chapter which mention each set of events. Once more we shall see how each point was predicted exactly. We shall again have the privilege of reading history which was written down *before it took place*!

Antiochus Epiphanes

21. In our previous chapter we learned how Antiochus the Great was followed by Seleucus Philopator, who mysteriously disappeared shortly after beginning to reign. The next person on the northern stage was also called Antiochus. He called

Daniel 11:21-45

himself 'Epiphanes' ('Illustrious'), but he was such an extraordinary character that his contemporaries referred to him as 'Epimanes' ('the Madman')!

A short list of adjectives can briefly summarize Antiochus' personality. He was cunning, powerful, cruel, foolish, greedy of gain, and immoral. Above all these things, he was a man of violent passions. This was the new king '... to whom they shall not give the honour of the kingdom'. Because he was not in succession to the throne, Antiochus was given no royal dignities. His path to the throne was the way of intrigue and smooth talking, as this verse accurately predicted.

22. It was not long before this new northern ruler was at war with the Ptolemies of Egypt, whom he utterly routed. At the same time he broke one of his closest allies, who is here referred to as 'the prince of the covenant'.

23. His next contact with Egypt was to make an alliance with it! Somehow he won the Egyptians' hearts, and this fact marks the real rise of Antiochus. From this point he became a rising star of increasing power and influence, although he had only 'a small people'.

24. Quite soon Antiochus Epiphanes was master of a lavish kingdom where he was able to dispense all sorts of riches to whomever he pleased. It was also a prodigal and immoral kingdom. His changed fortunes, however, did not change his ambitions. His heart was still set on the capture of 'the strongholds' of Egypt.

25-26. A new campaign was mounted against Egypt. Because of the treachery of some in their ranks, the Egyptians found it impossible to stand before him. The war resulted in an utter massacre. As the Seleucids advanced over the corpses of the Egyptians, did anyone recall this prophecy that 'many shall fall down slain'?

27. Eventually the two opposing kings met round a table. Our Lord had told Daniel, 'And both these kings shall be to do mischief, and they shall speak lies at one table ...' This is precisely what happened. Antiochus pretended that he would share power with Philometor who, in his turn, pretended to believe him! Each tried to pull the wool over the eyes of the other. But it was not yet God's appointed time for the wars between Egypt and Syria to come to an end. This is what the end of verse 27 means.

28-29. Antiochus returned home — rich, godless and apparently invincible; but in 168 B.C. he mounted yet another campaign against Egypt. 'But it shall not be as the former, or as the latter,' the Lord had said. This is a Hebrew way of saying that the new campaign was not going to have the success of the previous ones — which is exactly the way it was.

30. The reason for this was 'the ships of Chittim'. The reference is to the fleet of the prominent Roman soldier-cum-sailor, Popilius Laenas. On hearing of Antiochus' advance, he sailed at once for the Egyptian coast. The arrival of the Roman fleet so thoroughly disheartened Antiochus that he was prevented from taking Egypt and departed with rage and frustration for Palestine. Once there, he consulted with the Jews who had given up their faith and turned all his thoughts to the promised land.

31. He attacked Jerusalem, taking the women and children prisoner and securing the citadel overlooking the temple. There now began a systematic attempt to blot out every trace of Jewish religion and to introduce the thought and culture of the Greeks. There was no limit to Antiochus' attempt and savagery. His most repulsive act was to remove the temple's altar of burnt offering and to erect a pagan altar in its place.

32. By smooth talking, Antiochus persuaded the apostate Jews to become his allies and to forward his plans. But not all, by any means, were of such a mould. Within the nation there were still many men and women who knew God and who continued to walk with Him. A nameless mass of people were moved to countless acts of valour, rather than succumb to the pagan rites which Antiochus had made compulsory. Torture and martyrdom did not deter them either from personal piety or secret worship. A widespread resistance to Antiochus was quickly organized, and the time of oppression became a time of spiritual strength and memorable exploits for the persecuted remnant.

33. Spiritually perceptive men circulated secretly among the people, teaching them the Scriptures, leading them in prayer, and keeping alive the hope of the Messiah. The work continued unabated, although those that did it were relentlessly pursued and punished by the sword, the stake, imprisonment or impoverishment. The lengthy and cruel persecution was a period of much real faith and much true religion in the heart.

34. At last it looked as if the godly remnant could not hold out much longer. It was at this time that there took place the rebellion of the Maccabees. But Judas Maccabeus was not able to relieve the godly from all their distresses, especially as, out of fear of repercussions, many hypocrites associated with him and the faithful.

35. The time of persecution caused some who professed God's name to fall. For others it was a purifying and pruning experience and therefore a time of spiritual strengthening. Knowing that God would call a halt to it, in His own appointed time, they *never* gave in.

In this way our section covers the rise and activity of Antiochus Epiphanes. Once more we underline the wonder that such second-century events should have been predicted in the sixth century B.C. Many of the details of Daniel 11 were not known by historians until comparatively recently, and yet were perfectly predicted and recorded centuries beforehand. The supernatural origin of Scripture continues to encourage us, as do the lessons that God is unquestionably in control of all history, even when He is apparently nowhere to be seen. We have learned these lessons before, but we are so inclined to forget them that we are not ashamed to repeat them.

An important principle

So far we have studied chapter 11 only as far as verse 35. From verse 36 a strange thing happens to this chapter. It continues, it appears, to describe Antiochus Epiphanes. And yet it starts to say things that cannot be applied to him *in any way at all*!

Up until verse 35 the chapter has been historically perfect. Detail after detail has been predicted with breath-taking accuracy. From verse 36 there is no apparent change of subject. It seems as if it is still talking about the infamous Antiochus Epiphanes. And yet so many of the details simply do not, and indeed *cannot*, fit him. When we get to the beginning of chapter 12, which is a continuation of the same vision, we find that it is the end of the world that is being spoken about! There is mention of the resurrection and the destinies of everlasting life and everlasting contempt.

What shall we make of all this? It is as if the prophet, in

seeing Antiochus Epiphanes, looks through him and sees him as a type or prefigurement of *somebody else like him* who is to come in the future.

This should not really surprise us very much. We should remember that in chapter 7 Daniel saw 'a little horn'. That 'little horn' was an evil figure who is going to come at the end of the world, and who will cause the people of God to suffer as they have done before.

In chapter 8 we saw that Antiochus Epiphanes, of whom we have just been reading again, was also described as 'a little horn'. Two distinct individuals were given the same description in two consecutive chapters of the same book. One was a person who has now lived and died. The other is yet to come. We saw that both are given the same description because, in a sense, they are in fact the same.

We learned that the final Antichrist will be preceded by many previous antichrists. History is full of prominent individuals who have set themselves up and have tried to put the people of God down. They are forerunners of the final Antichrist. When one of them comes onto the scene, it is all but impossible to know whether he is just one more antichrist, or whether he is *the* Antichrist. When you are being spitefully opposed by such a person, you can be forgiven for thinking that your oppressor is the final Antichrist. It is not until subsequent events prove that he is not that you can be aware of your mistake. At the time there is no shame in considering that he may well be that final and awful individual whose coming heralds the last hours of human history. It is plain that to a godly man or woman two distinct individuals can, in fact, look as if they are *one*!

If that is a fact of Christian experience, we should not be surprised to discover that it is also a fact of prophetic experience. As he looks into the future, the prophet may well see two distinct individuals as one, and his prophecy may go naturally from one to the other. Many of the prophets not only did this with future personalities, but also with future events. Subsequent history displayed that the two sets of events were distinct, but in predicting them, while giving hints about their distinction, the prophet spoke about them as one. If we cannot grasp this feature of prophecy, our understanding of it will always be limited.

It is precisely this feature that we witness in Daniel 11. The Lord causes Daniel to look through Antiochus Epiphanes to the person of whom he is a prefigurement — the man of sin. From verse 36 Daniel is still, in a way, talking about Antiochus. But he is most certainly talking most about the Antichrist, for things are said here which cannot in any way apply to Antiochus. With this clearly in our minds we now take up our study again from verse 36.

The man of sin

36. Verse 36 tells us of a king who will do exactly what he wants. The picture is of a man coming to power, prospering, increasing in power, and now speaking against every god. It is true that Antiochus Epiphanes assumed divinity, but he never did *that*, for throughout his life he maintained some form of religion. He spoke against the God of gods, but never against all religion. The only fulfilment of this verse must be in him 'who opposeth and exalteth himself above all that is called God, or that is worshipped ...' (2 Thessalonians 2:4).

Once we are clear that the chapter is now referring mostly to someone beyond Antiochus Epiphanes, our interpretation of each individual phrase is affected. Much Old Testament prophecy uses literal language but, as the apostles' interpretation of it shows, that literal language is not to be pressed. In speaking of eschatological events the prophets used the only language open to them. But that language was too limited to describe adequately the prophetic events to which they referred. Their literal language must therefore be given a fuller and more exalted significance than the words themselves allow.

37. It would be embarrassing to refer verse 37 to Antiochus. The person of this verse has no regard for any god whatsoever, which, we say again, was simply not true of him. The picture here is of a man trampling on what his fathers valued, a person without human love and without any piety of any sort at all.

38–39. The only god whom this person worships is *force*. To this he devotes everything, and with its help he will proceed against his enemies and will dispense rewards to those who are on his side.

40. The time will come when there will be two opponents face to face. On the one hand there will be a king typified by Antiochus Epiphanes, and here called 'the king of the north'. On the other hand will be one typified by the Ptolemies, and here called 'the king of the south'. Those will be days of battle, when the Antichrist will be preoccupied with the quest for territorial extension.

41. He will defeat all who withstand him, and the only people who will escape his wrath will be those who are already the enemies of the people of God.

Verse 41 cannot possibly refer to anything to do with Antiochus because it refers to the nation of Moab. That nation no longer existed in Antiochus' time and does not exist today. It is plain, therefore, that this verse cannot be interpreted literally, although its language has a literal form.

Edom, Moab and Ammon are the traditional enemies of the people of God. As we cannot interpret them literally, we must spritualize what is taught here — as we so often have to do with Old Testament prophecy. We take this to be a figurative reference that when the Antichrist comes the only ones who will escape his venom will be those who are already in opposition to God's people.

42–44. Nowhere in the whole world will escape from his fury. He will be an all-conquering force, commanding universal submission. Rebellion will be impossible, for whenever he will hear a rumour of it, he will put it down.

45. At last he will set up his throne on sacred and holy ground, 'so that he as God sitteth in the temple of God, showing himself that he is God' (2 Thessalonians 2:4), as Paul puts it.

You may not agree with me, but I am satisfied in my own mind that from verses 21 to 45 we have a vision of Antiochus Epiphanes which merges into a vision of a final and horrifying eschatological figure, who quickly becomes the only figure in the chapter. The chapter closes with the comforting assurance that 'He shall come to his end, and none shall help him.'

A serious approach

I do not expect all who read this book to be in total agreement with the interpretation which has been given. Please feel free to dissent from the interpretation — provided you can come up with a better one! But none of us is free to dissent from the truth that a personal Antichrist will come at the end of the world, and this should give our Christian lives an element of real seriousness.

The Word of God makes it plain that the last day *cannot come* unless there is first a falling away, and there takes place the revealing of the 'man of sin ... the son of perdition' (2 Thessalonians 2:3).

There are some who nurse prophetic views which lead them to believe that the whole world will at least be 'Christianized'. They dream of the day when every government, institution, factory and school is powerfully affected by Christian influence. They long for the golden days which are ahead. Such dreamers are going to be very disappointed indeed. Evil men are going to get worse and worse (2 Timothy 3:13) until there comes an evil individual of such wickedness as the world has never seen before.

When that person comes we will see that the many other 'little horns' of history were nothing but his forerunners. He will be worse than anybody who has previously existed, and his persecution of the people of God will be unprecedented.

This is why we plead for a serious approach to the Christian life. This is why we are against the frivolity and shallowness which characterizes so much contemporary Christianity. There are awful days ahead for the Christian church — worse than anything that has gone before. There are going to be martyrs again. Nobody should embark on the Christian life without calling these facts to mind and without counting the cost.

We will be better prepared for those days if we can learn from this chapter a lesson which we have already learned several times in our studies of the book of Daniel. It is that nothing happens without the approval of our heavenly Father. *History is in God's hands.*

Verses 27, 29 and 35 all refer to 'the time appointed' or 'a time appointed'. Verse 36 tells us 'that that is determined shall be done'. When all history appears to be out of control, God still has His hands on the reins. If that were not so, He would not *be* God!

It is because His control is absolute that the predictions of this chapter could be made. The same is true of the promise at the end of verse 45. It is because God rules in history that we can be sure, not only that the Antichrist will come, but also that he will come to his end.

The chapter should also encourage us to realize that *no amount of persecution can hinder our communion with God.* In the darkest times, 'The people that do know their God shall be strong and do exploits' (32).

Cruel oppressors can close down all public worship and forbid all Christian meetings. They can take away our printed Bibles and our Christian books. They can outlaw Christian work, remove all our liberties, threaten us with cruel penalties and allow the Lord's people no visible presence whatever. But they cannot take away our communion with God. They cannot stop us knowing God. Even modern mind-bending drugs have been found to be unable to remove all enjoyment of the comfort of His presence. There are some things that evil forces, however unrestrained, cannot do. This is why there will always be a remnant. Even in the darkest times there will always be those who go among others teaching them the truth of God. No oppression has served to do anything except, ultimately, to further the spread of gospel truth. God's plants do not thrive in greenhouses — but in wind, hail, snow and burning heat.

Even that lesson is not the end of the encouragement which this chapter has to offer us. It also shows us again that *we can be certain that evil will not finally triumph.*

Let us think again of Antiochus Epiphanes. When he came to power it seemed as if it was the end of all true faith. Palestine was the only country on earth where true believers were to be found, and that was the very place where he was let loose. His campaign of extermination seemed certain to succeed. But it did not. He did not wipe out the faith.

What happened to him? Filled with ambition to conquer Persia, he left Lysias to deal with the Maccabees, and set off towards his goal. However his ambition was frustrated because the Persians had been forewarned.

Antiochus had intended to steal considerable amounts of treasure from Persia and to use it to fund a campaign against Babylon. Instead, he had to proceed without it. On his way to Babylon he received news that at home his own general had

Daniel 11:21-45

been defeated by the Maccabees and that an altar to Jehovah had once more been erected in the temple of Jerusalem.

It had proved impossible to defeat Antiochus in battle, to assassinate him or to destroy him politically. But when this seemingly invincible man heard this news, he felt so ill that he went to bed, where he died in terror and dismay. God blew on him, and he went!

It has been the same with every antichrist, and will be the same again with the final one. In thinking of his arrogance and power we should not forget that he is nothing more than the one 'whom the Lord shall consume with the spirit of his mouth, and shall destroy with the brightness of his coming' (2 Thessalonians 2:8).

'Praise our God, all ye his servants, and ye that fear him, both small and great ... Alleluia: for the Lord God omnipotent reigneth' (Revelation 19:5-6).

15.
THE END!

Please read Daniel chapter 12

The fourteen-year-old boy that we met in chapter 1 is now an old man of eighty-six or eighty-seven. Throughout the long years he has dared to stand alone for God in a hostile environment. He has clearly shown to us that the spiritual life does not require ideal conditions in which to thrive and flourish. In any event, there are no ideal circumstances anywhere. The godly life can grow and develop in the darkest and most difficult places. So it is that he who walked with the Lord in the morning of his life walks even more closely with Him in the evening.

By the River Tigris our Lord Jesus Christ has appeared to His faithful prophet and has given him a vision of the main milestones of history for several hundred years to follow. But the Lord has done more than that. He has caused the old man's eyes to look into the very distant future, too, and at the end of chapter 11 Daniel gazed at a wicked individual who is to appear at the end of the world. This person will be entirely godless and invincibly powerful throughout the world. He will inflict unimaginable and unprecedented persecution upon the people of God and, 'yet he shall come to his end, and none shall help him' (11:45).

The end of the world

The first four verses of our present chapter are part of that same vision and continue to reveal what will happen during those very last days.

They begin by assuring us that even *that* dark period of world history, with all its horrors for God's people, will be bounded on all sides by the angels of God! History will be no

Daniel 12

more out of control at that time than at any other time. Heaven will continue to hold the reins of what is happening on earth. At the very time that there is distress such as no nation has ever seen, the archangel Michael will stand up to protect the people of God, to take their side and to deliver them (1).

The Bible is quite clear that at that time all hell will be let loose against the church of Jesus Christ. But that is not all. 'At that time thy people shall be delivered, everyone that shall be found written in the book.'

The names of God's people are written in a book. It is to that book that Jesus referred when He said, 'In this rejoice not, that the spirits are subject unto you; but rather rejoice, because your names are written in heaven' (Luke 10:20). It is to the same book that John referred in the Revelation, when he wrote of the last judgement: 'And whosoever was not found written in the book of life was cast into the lake of fire' (Revelation 20:15).

There is a book with individual names in it. They are the names of those whom God has everlastingly loved and given to His Son. They are the sheep for whom the shepherd died and whom His Spirit has called to savingly believe. It is these people, whose names are recorded in heaven, who are going to enjoy the glorious deliverance mentioned in the opening verse of this final chapter.

When the end of the world comes, there will be nothing else that will really matter, except whether our names are in that book. Our reputation and achievements among men and women will be of no more importance. Our possessions will all have been destroyed in the great conflagration. Only our acceptance with God will matter.

The day of the overthrow of Antichrist (11:45) will also be the day when our Lord will descend from heaven with a shout, with the voice of the archangel and with the sound of God's trumpet (1 Thessalonians 4:16). It is then that the events of verse 2 will take place: 'And many of them that sleep in the dust of the earth shall awake, some to everlasting life, and some to shame and everlasting contempt.'

The last day is to be resurrection day. Deliverance from death is not guaranteed to persecuted Christians, but deliverance *out of* death is a certainty. We should not be confused by the use of the word 'many' in verse 2. It is a Hebrew way of drawing attention to the vastness of the numbers involved, but does not mean anything less than 'all'. But the fact that all are going to rise does not mean that all will enjoy the same sort of resurrection. Resurrection day will also be division day. The King in His glory will divide the members of the human race from one another, as a shepherd divides his sheep from the goats (Matthew 25:32). No grave will fail to give up its dead (John 5:28-29). Wherever the dead have been laid, they will be summoned to the great assize (Revelation 20:13). At Christ's word each member of the human race will pass to one or the other of two destinies: 'some to everlasting life, and some to shame and everlasting contempt'.

The Bible has a great deal to say about the eternal punishment of the wicked, but in this chapter the emphasis is upon the reward into which loyal believers will enter (3). This is because the book of Daniel was written primarily with such believers in mind. But who precisely *are* the 'wise' of verse 3? Who *are* those 'that turn many to righteousness'?

To understand this we must cast back our minds to 11:33. There we read that in the darkest days of Antiochus Epiphanes' persecution there were those who circulated among the people, instructing them in God's truth. They not only continued to believe, but they also did everything in their power to spread the truth — although hounded, imprisoned, tortured and murdered.

During the unspeakable persecutions of the final apostasy there will be similar 'wise' people who 'turn many to righteousness'. Come what may, they will continue to believe, and will continue also with the work of God. When all hell is let loose, they will not give up. Will it be worth it? They, and all others who did similar exploits in previous days, will not lose their eternal reward. The sufferings of the present time will not be worth comparing with the glory which they will enjoy. Days of divine reward and eternal brightness await them. For keeping the light shining in the darkest hour they shall 'shine as the brightness of the firmament' and 'as the stars for ever and ever.'

Measured by human logic, their work was foolishness. This is the estimate that the unconverted world always puts upon the spreading of the gospel message, so how much more so when the days are fiercely dark? When all their enemies are confounded in their shame, and sentenced to everlasting contempt, it will be seen how very wise these preachers of righteousness have been. There will be nothing transient about their reward. It will be for ever and ever:

> When we've been there a thousand years,
> Bright shining as the sun,
> We've no less days to sing God's praise
> Than when we first begun.

'Seal all this up, Daniel,' says our Lord in verse 4. 'These are the things that I have unveiled to you in the vision. Now seal it up.'

This does not mean that the things revealed to Daniel were to remain a secret. The old Persian custom was that once a book had been copied and publicly circulated, one copy was sealed and placed in the library. This was so that future generations could read it. It is important to note that was done only once the book had begun to enjoy a wide readership.

Daniel's last prophetic act was thus to ensure that what was revealed to him was known, not only by his own generation, but by generations to come. It is not God's will that men and women of any time should be ignorant of the final outcome of history. He wants all to know what lies ahead.

For all this, 'many shall run to and fro, and knowledge shall be increased' (4). What the future holds is laid up in the book that we have open. Despite this, men and women are restless in their pursuit of knowledge and run hither and thither to obtain it. Never before have people had access to so much knowledge as they do today. Yet ignorance of the future is as widespread as ever. In all their hope and fear, men and women have proved quite unable to guess what lies ahead. It cannot be known except by revelation from God, and what we most need to know is revealed to us by our Lord in this book.

It is Christ who will end the world. He will throw down the Antichrist, raise, judge and divide the dead, and consign us all to our eternal destinies. The only people who will enter into His eternal reward will be those who took God's side, even when it was a difficult side to take.

And one of those who will enter into that reward will be a person who, when he was fourteen, resolved never to displease God and tried to live the whole of his long life by that great principle. He found nothing easy about such a course of action, yet it was worth it. The humble author of this Old Testament book will be one of those who 'shine as the brightness of the firmament' and 'as the stars for ever and ever'.

The end of the book

The lengthy vision given to Daniel by the River Tigris ends at verse 4. From verse 5 we study a further scene, which closes the book.

The Lord Jesus Christ has, of course, been with Daniel throughout the time that He has been revealing the future to him. But now He is joined by two others, heavenly visitors, one on the nearside bank and one on the river bank opposite (5).

The Lord Himself is not on either bank, but upon the water (6). Was His walking on the water during the period of the Gospels intended to draw attention to this passage, and to identify Him as the One who spoke with Daniel? As Daniel watches and listens, he hears one of the recently arrived angels ask his Lord a question: 'How long shall it be to the end of these wonders?' The angel is enquiring when the events predicted of the end of the world will take place.

'The man clothed in linen,' who is our pre-incarnate Lord, replies by lifting up both His hands (7). To raise one hand is, in the Old Testament, the sign of a solemn oath. To raise both means that the oath is exceptionally solemn. Our Lord Jesus Christ replies to the enquiry by thus raising both His hands, and swearing by Himself, 'by him that liveth for ever'.

And what is His answer? 'That it shall be for time, times, and an half' (7).

This is exactly the same information, given in Hebrew, as was given in Aramaic in 7:25. There it was said of the coming Antichrist, 'And he shall speak great words against the most High, and shall wear out the saints of the most High, and think to change times and laws: and they shall be given into his hand until a time and times and the dividing of time.'

What does that mean? We will interpret it just as we did before. It does not say, 'Year, years and half a year'; the talk is of 'times'. The Antichrist will dominate the world for a time. When it seems that he has gone on as long as it is possible to do so, he will continue to dominate the world for *twice* that time. It will then appear as if he is going to continue for twice *that* time. It will seem as if he is going to go on for ever.

It is precisely at that point that he will be cut down — at the very height of his power, and at the very peak of his influence. By then he will have practically destroyed God's people, 'and when he shall have accomplished to scatter the power of the holy people, all these things shall be finished' (7).

If I properly understand Revelation chapter 11 and its narrative relating to the two witnesses, the days are coming when the church of Christ will be utterly broken by evil power. We will come to the point in history where it appears that darkness has really won the day. It will seem as if the Antichrist is going to continue for ever. It will seem as if the church has been entirely obliterated, for there will no longer be any sign of it.

All this we have said before. And we say this again, too — it is at *that* time that the Antichrist will be broken — once, for all, and for ever.

That is why we should not despair when we see wickedness increasing. Evil will not be broken when it is at a low ebb, but when it is at its *height*!

All this Daniel heard, but he was still confused (8). 'Then said I, O my Lord, what shall be the end of these things?'

This is not a mere echo of the angel's question in verse 6, for Daniel uses a different Hebrew word for 'end' in his question. Hearing of the evil days ahead, his question is for information about the *closing stages* of that period. The evil days described are reserved for the end of the world. What will be the sign that those dark days are coming to their final close?

'Do not ask anything more, Daniel,' comes the divine reply. 'Leave the matter alone. Enquire no further, "for the words are closed up and sealed till the time of the end"' (9).

In other words, what has been revealed is reserved for the days of which it spoke. It is not necessary for Daniel to understand completely everything that has been said, because not all of it had immediate application to him and his time. But when the words need to be understood, they will be understood.

This reply illustrates to us the practical nature of Holy Scripture. The Bible has not been given to us to satisfy our curiosity, but to bring us to faith, to sustain us in that faith, and to bring us more fully into the image of Christ. It is given to sanctify us and to change our lives. Answering our speculations has never been part of its purpose.

We must realize that some of the Bible's teachings relating to the very last days will not be understood until we are *in* those days. That is why it is both unwise and dangerous to draw up detailed timetables of future events. Some parts of the Word of God will not become obvious in their meaning until the days of which they speak have dawned.

Personally I find this teaching very comforting, especially in considering such verses as 11 and 12 of this chapter. You will see in a few moments that I cannot tell you what they mean. I do not have a clue. But I believe that we shall understand them well enough when we need to.

Before we look at those two verses we must consider our Lord's words in verse 10. What do they mean? They are a prediction of coming persecutions. People are going to be purified, made white and tried. The church of Christ is going to undergo a pruning process. It is at that time that what is revealed will be understood. The wicked will continue with their wickedness, and will not understand, because they are not spiritually discerning. But the wise shall understand. What Daniel could not understand at the moment of revelation, what we cannot understand after centuries of study — the wise shall understand *then*.

When those awful days burst upon the church of Christ, how glad the believers of those days will be that they knew chapter 12! What will sustain them when all hell is let loose? The Bible! The plain, old-fashioned pages of the Word of God! The words which none of us have hitherto understood will be to them a source of blessing, comfort and strength. How glad they will be that they never forsook the Word of God for 'other things'!

As it is, up until now, nobody anywhere has been able to understand verse 11. Every attempt to do so has failed. It talks of 1290 days, and in speaking of the coming Antichrist our Lord here uses language which is more suited to Antiochus Epiphanes.

At thirty days to the month, 1290 days equals three and a half years, plus one month. I have no idea what it means. This does not make me ashamed, for I am confident that you do not understand it either! But this I know — whatever comes upon us, we are in the hands of God. No days come upon the church of Christ without divine appointment. God has set a limit on those days, and they will not continue for one day longer than the limit He has set. Therefore, although I do not understand what 1290 days means, I do believe that I understand the gist and the thrust of the verse. Whatever may be the persecution that breaks upon God's people, it will go on for a definite time, and when that definite time is over, it will cease!

'Hang on,' says verse 12, 'Hang on! Don't give in! Up until 1335 days. Hang on for forty-five days more!'

I do not know what that means either. But I know this — that when the Christian church enters into the period of its final and worst persecution, those days will not go on for ever. They may go on for a long time, but there are divinely decreed limits to them. At last the persecution will reach an intensity that it cannot exceed, and then it will end.

We are to hang on during periods of persecution, because the Christian church has never yet entered a tunnel to which there was no end. Very often the tunnel has been darker and longer than anyone dared to imagine, but those who held on to their faith despite everything eventually burst out into the sunshine again. In the case of the final persecution, the sunshine will be that of the Saviour's exaltation at the end of the world.

Paul speaks about this subject in 2 Timothy 3. It is a chapter about 'the last days' — a phrase which is always used biblically to denote the period between Christ's first coming and His second. He tells us that in those last days there will be 'perilous times' (1). The Greek word used means that he is referring to seasons in history when there will be great unleashings of evil. The period between Christ's two comings will be characterized by waves and outbreaks of wickedness.

He then tells us that the wicked men of those evil seasons 'shall proceed no further' (9). To every period of unloosed iniquity there is a decreed end. Every tunnel has an end, and this is true of the last tunnel, too. Whenever we experience a great unloosing of evil forces, there is no way of knowing whether this is just one of many such waves, or whether it is the final apostasy. But we do not need to know. Whatever it is, it will have an end. Our duty begins and ends by remembering the words of the Lord Jesus Christ: 'He that shall endure unto the end, the same shall be saved' (Matthew 24:13).

The exhortation to hold on a little longer is followed by the last verse of this great book: 'But go thy way,' continues the Lord, 'till the end be.'

We must not conjure up a mental picture of a parent telling his child to 'run along now'. These are not words of dismissal. The verse does not mean, 'Daniel, go away now, for I have finished giving you revelation', but rather, 'Daniel, go on in the spiritual life, as you *are* going.'

Even the old prophet needed to be reminded to persevere! But then he is told, 'For thou shalt rest, and stand in thy lot at the end of the days.'

Daniel, so faithful through so many years, is to go on in the spiritual life until he dies. Soon he will rest in the grave. But that will not be the end of him. After that rest, he will enter into his reward. What is laid up for him will finally be his, and he will enter into the enjoyment of it.

No doubt this Old Testament believer did not see things as clearly as we who have the benefit of New Covenant revelation. But how encouraging these words must have been to him! The Lord did not let him leave this mortal life without the certain assurance of a reward to follow. What a consolation to him who throughout his life had loved his Lord first, and had therefore dared to stand alone! No one who lives in a godly way escapes persecution and trouble in this life. The environment is always hostile. Yet, equally certainly, no one who lives in a godly way misses the rewards of heaven.

> Soon shall come the great awakening;
> Soon the rending of the tomb;
> Then the scattering of all shadows,
> And the end of toil and gloom.

Thank You

— To the Rev. James Philip, of Holyrood Abbey Church of Scotland, Edinburgh. Mr Philip's lively and practical commentary on Daniel, *By the Rivers of Babylon* (Didasko Press), was the first book that ever moved me to read Daniel with enthusiasm. I have leaned very heavily on it as I have written the preceding pages, and I am grateful to Mr Philip for kind permission to have done so.

— To the Banner of Truth Trust for permission to lean equally heavily on *A Commentary on Daniel* by the late Professor E.J. Young. Without these two crutches, how could I have made any progress? In Professor Young we see sanctified scholarship at its best. His learning was profound, but his presentation of his material comparatively simple. All serious students of the Bible should have his work on their shelf, and beside it should be *Studies in the Book of Daniel* by the late, and equally lamented, Professor Robert Dick Wilson.

— To Miss Lynn Webb of Gunningbland, New South Wales, Australia. Lynn used weeks of her spare time to listen to a series of my recorded messages on Daniel, and then to type them all out for me, word for word. The arrival of that material was the final motivation that I needed to start on a written coverage of the same ground.

— To the elders, deacons and members of Belvidere Road Church, Liverpool, my immediate travelling companions on the narrow road to life. For a year they released me from half of my pastoral responsibilities, so that I could have more time to write; and they prayed that such a course of action might be of benefit to the wider cause of Christ. May He who rules in heaven and on earth be pleased to grant their request!

The Gospel as it Really is
Paul's Epistle to the Romans simply explained

Stuart Olyott

Perhaps no other book has had as profound an influence on the history of the Christian church as Paul's Epistle to the Romans. It was the discovery of the real message of Romans by Martin Luther which caused him to break away from the church of Rome and become a leader of the Reformation. Many others, before and since, among them Augustine, John Bunyan and John Wesley, have owed their conversion to the teaching of this epistle.

Luther said of Romans: 'It can never be read or considered too much or too well, and the more it is handled, the more delightful it becomes and the better it tastes.'

In this book the author aims to present a simple introduction to Romans for the ordinary reader. His exposition goes straight to the heart of the passage, avoiding technicalities or obscure textual criticism.

Alive in Christ
Ephesians simply explained

Stuart Olyott

When we begin to understand Paul's Epistle to the Ephesians, something wonderful happens to our spiritual life. Realizing how rich we are in Christ, we become filled with thankfulness and joy. We never envy non-Christians again. We see what it means to live as a Christian in today's world. We become stable in our doctrinal understanding. In short, Ephesians produces exactly the sort of Christians we most need.

That is why this short commentary has been written. It is for those who want to begin to understand Paul's great letter. More advanced believers will find spiritual refreshment here. May a fresh reading of Ephesians help all of us to 'grow up in all things into him who is the head — Christ'! (Eph. 4:15)

A Life Worth Living and a Lord Worth Loving
Ecclesiastes & Song of Solomon

Stuart Olyott

Has life really got any meaning? Our time in this world is comparatively short. The earthly stage remains, but different actors are constantly passing across it. Generations come and go, but nothing is ultimately different.

This is how many people see life, and Solomon identifies with them. But is life really pointless? If not, what is its true meaning?

The message of Ecclesiastes is that life is not worth living unless we live it for God. The Song of Solomon teaches us that living for the Lord means loving him.

As in his other popular commentaries, Stuart Olyott gives a heart-warming and practical explanation of the message of these two Old Testament books. They are books full of meaning and challenge for today.